Battle at
ALCATRAZ

A Desperate Attempt to Escape the Rock

Ernest B. Lageson

Addicus Books, Inc.
Omaha, Nebraska

An Addicus Nonfiction Book

ISBN# 1-886039-37-2

Cover design by Jeff Reiner, Tim Young
Typography by Linda Dageforde
Illustrations by Bob Hogenmiller

Library of Congress Cataloging-in-Publication Data

Lageson, Ernest B., 1932-
    Battle at Alcatraz : a desperate attempt to escape the rock / Ernest B. Lageson.
cm.
        Includes bibliographical references (p.).
        ISBN 1-886039-37-2 (alk. paper)
        1. United States Penitentiary, Alcatraz Island, California. Prison riots. California. Case studies. I. Title.
    HV9474.A4L34   1999
    365'.641.dc21
                                                                98-41824
                                                                CIP
                        Addicus Books, Inc.
                        P.O. Box 45327
                        Omaha, Nebraska 68145
                Web site: http://www.AddicusBooks.com

Printed in the United States of America

10 9 8

To the memory of my father, who has been a source of inspiration and a role model for me all my life.

Author's Notes

Battle at Alcatraz should have been written by my father, Ernie Lageson Sr. He is the one who lived the incredible experience. However, his untimely death intervened, so I have written this account in tribute to him.

My father worked as a custodial officer at Alcatraz between 1942 and 1948, with a brief hiatus while he served in the Navy during World War II. He was the officer in charge of the cell house on that fateful day in 1946 when the bloody insurrection occurred. He was taken hostage, shot, and left for dead for several hours before he was rescued. Later, he was also one of the key witnesses at the murder trial of the surviving rioters. A great deal of the information I used in writing this book came directly from my father.

Additionally, I did extensive research over the

five years that I worked on this book. I scoured hundreds of newspaper articles covering the riot and the trial. I reviewed extensive portions of the FBI investigation file, including over a hundred statements from officers and prisoners. I also studied more than 2,500 pages of trial transcripts, hundreds of pages of court files, trial briefs, court opinions, and related documents. Most of the scenes and dialogue in the book are based on these documents.

I also interviewed former officers and former inmate Jim Quillan, who served time at Alcatraz in 1946. I had a brief meeting with Clarence Carnes, the only surviving inmate participant in the riot. My research also included in-depth interviews with Archer Zamloch, who represented Carnes at the trial.

Finally, some of the material for this book is based on my own memories. I lived in civilian quarters on Alcatraz Island when I was a boy of thirteen. Through my father, I met most of the custodial personnel depicted in this book. I was also the newspaper boy on Alcatraz Island, so I knew most of the residents from having delivered Bay Area newspapers to them.

Acknowledgments

A considerable number of people assisted me in preparing this book. I am sincerely grateful to them all.

First and foremost, I wish to recognize the contribution of my father, who not only lived the dramatic riot in May 1946 but also generously shared his recollections with me.

I am also grateful for the help of other members of my family. My daughter Kristine Cardall provided invaluable aid as my editor. Without her work, I probably would still be struggling with a rewrite. My son Ernie assisted with graphics and the artistic aspects of the work. Finally, my wife Jeanne contributed her thoughts, time, and encouragement to help make the whole thing happen.

I am appreciative of the research support I received from the staff at the National Archives in San

Bruno, California, particularly from Neil Thomsen, Lisa Miller, and Claude Hopkins. I also wish to thank Michael Griffith, archivist for the U.S. District Court; Irene Stachura, librarian; and Bill Kooiman of the National Maritime Museum. Thanks, too, to the staffs of the San Francisco, Berkeley, Oakland, University of California, and Boalt Hall School of Law libraries for facilitating my research. I also thank Jennie Peuron for sharing with me her research on Sam Shockley, part of her work in writing the play Crazy Sam. Chuck Stucker, the son of Ed Stucker and himself a former resident of the island, provided a great deal of help with photographs as well as general support and encouragement.

The park rangers of the Golden Gate National Recreation Area, particularly John Cantwell, were extraordinarily cooperative and allowed me unlimited access to various Alcatraz venues. They are a dedicated group of professionals who do a wonderful job.

Special thanks go to a number of individuals who gave freely of their time and recollection. The following persons greatly assisted my research: the late Jim Quillan, an author and former inmate who was confined in D Block at the time of the riot; Mrs. Kay Sullivan, the widow of attorney William Sullivan, who defended Sam Shockley in his murder trial; Mrs. Annette Newmark, the widow of Aaron Vinkler, one of the attorneys for Miran Thompson; Lois Vinkler and Hermine Simon, the daughters of Aaron Vinkler; Archer Zamloch, the attorney who defended Clarence Carnes; George Finnigan, former law part-ncr of Aaron Vinkler and longtime San Francisco practitioner; the late Judge Joseph Karesh, former assistant U.S. attorney and counsel for the Alcatraz administration; Jeannie Comerford Campbell; and Donald Martin, a close friend of my father and former Alcatraz custodial officer.

Finally, I wish to thank my longtime friend and widely acclaimed writer, Ron Fimrite, for his time and editorial comment.

Prologue

Alcatraz inmate Bernard "Bernie" Coy lay on his bunk, smoking and staring into the semidarkness of his five-by-nine-foot cell 155. As the harsh smoke from the hand-rolled Bull Durham cigarette filled his lungs, he contemplated what was about to become the single biggest event in his long and violent criminal career. Today he would lead a blastout from Alcatraz that would overshadow everything he had done in his life and make him one of the most famous inmates in the history of the island prison. Tomorrow his name and picture would be on the front page of every major newspaper in America and, given the public interest in Alcatraz, his fame might even reach international proportions.

Coy had dreamed about escaping for years. His active planning had gone on for months. He believed everything was now in place. He knew every move of all the cell-house officers and where they normally were at all times of the day. He knew the numbers and locations of all the critical keys. The tools he would need were in place and ready. The timing had been planned in great detail. The people were set. It had to work. There was no way it would fail.

Coy thought again about his hand-picked gang and how carefully he had selected them. Each was tough and courageous. Buddy Thompson and Marv Hubbard were solid. Both had shot it out with the police in the past. Coy was sure he could count on them. Hubbard, in particular, had demonstrated tremendous courage in police gunfights against tremendous odds and in many cases had escaped. Thompson, the Texas cop killer, was cool and self-assured, not easily excited or rattled. Coy wondered about the Indian kid, though. Joe Carnes was only eighteen years old, doing life for murder and kidnapping. How would he react if things really got tough? Coy had studied the young convict closely for months but had only recently told him of the breakout plans. Carnes was eager to be a part of it. Coy was satisfied that he could at least count on the youngster to do what he was told.

The fourth man Coy had picked was Joe Cretzer. He was an accomplished gunman and had attempted breakouts from McNeil Island and Alcatraz. He killed a U.S. marshal while trying to escape from a federal courtroom during one of his trials. As one of the most violent and successful bank robbers of his time, Cretzer had been Number Five on J. Edgar Hoover's list of the ten most-wanted criminals in America. Coy's only concern about Cretzer was how he would react to a sudden emergency. Would he be cool, or would he go crazy and start shooting? Joe was tough and a bit of a hothead, but Coy believed he could control the dapper San Francisco bank robber.

Sitting up, Coy crushed out his cigarette and lit another. Tomorrow, he thought, I'll be smoking Lucky Strikes or maybe a Cuban cigar and drinking good Kentucky whiskey. No more of this roll-your-own Bull Durham shit.

Coy glanced around his cell, dimly lit by the ceiling lights in the cell house. He studied the oil paintings he had done over the years, carefully displayed in the rear corner of his tiny cubicle. His gaze lingered on the landscape he had done of the hills near his birthplace of New Haven, Kentucky. It was a peaceful scene. Coy thought briefly of his youth and how he had enjoyed roaming those hills. Often he had gone off by himself, living off the land and sleeping under the stars. In fact, his last days of freedom had been spent in the hills outside New Haven. Coy and his cronies robbed the Bank of New Haven, Kentucky, then took refuge in a cave along the Rolling Fork River. They were prepared to live off the land and the supplies they had previously hidden. But they were surprised one night a few days after the holdup by a posse and were captured without a fight.

And there was the portrait of his wife he had painted several years earlier. He had not seen Peggy in nearly ten years. It had been years since he received any mail from her. He wondered where she was and if he would ever see her again. When I get to Frisco, Coy thought, maybe I'll give her a call. I might even go back to Kentucky to see her and the rest of my family.

He picked up his steel mirror and moved to the front of his cell. Holding the mirror outside the bars, Coy viewed the corridor in each direction. It was empty except for a couple of guards chatting quietly down at Times Square, preparing for the wake-up count. Returning to his bunk, the slender, wiry Coy thought to himself that the cell house seemed unusually quiet. By early afternoon, he mused, there will be plenty of action.

1

Ernie Lageson stepped out of the shower. He had a gnawing feeling in the pit of his stomach. He could sense trouble brewing in the Alcatraz cell house where he worked as a guard. Nothing he could put his finger on, really, but the inmates had been far too quiet. Something was brewing.

He glanced at the clock. Almost 5:45 A.M. Time to get moving. He slipped into his officer's uniform—a freshly starched gray shirt, gray trousers and jacket, and black tie. He quickly buffed his already shining shoes, a longtime habit reinforced by his recent Navy duty.

Ernie went to the kitchen to join his wife and son for breakfast. The family of three made their home in a modest apartment on the top floor of a three-story apartment building on Sacramento Street, between Franklin and Van Ness, in San Francisco. The breakfast conversation quickly turned to baseball. Thirteen-year-old Ernie Jr. was a great fan of the San Francisco Seals and followed the local team and the Triple-A Pacific Coast League closely. San Francisco was leading the league by three games over arch-rival Oakland and was four games ahead of the Los Angeles Angels. Tonight they were playing the Angels in the third game of a seven-game series. The Seals had lost the last two games.

Ernie Sr. couldn't resist a little playful teasing, even though he, too, was a Seals fan, especially of Seals manager Lefty O'Doul.

"Looks like L.A.'s got the Seals on the run, Pal. If the Seals drop tonight's game, that'll be three losses in a row. Looks like a three-way race to me. Both Oakland and L.A. are coming on stronger than the Seals."

"Don't worry, Dad. Ray Harrell is pitching tonight and Cliff Melton on Friday night. Besides, two losses in a row is freaky, the first time it's happened all year."

"I'm not worrying, Son. It's you Seals fans who have to worry," Ernie laughed.

Listening to Ernie Sr. and their son banter, Eunice Lageson hadn't said anything. She sipped the last of her coffee and sighed. "It's time for me to leave," she said. She kissed both Ernies as she left to catch her bus to her clerical job in the alcohol tax section of the Treasury Department.

Young Ernie washed the breakfast dishes—one of his regular chores—then hustled out the door for school. "See you tonight, Dad," he called and went downstairs, hurrying to catch the H Car, the first of the streetcars that took him to Marina Junior High School.

Just before he, too, left the apartment, Ernie Sr. took the eight-inch, leather blackjack that hung on the back of the bedroom door and slipped it into a special pocket sewn into his right trouser leg. Firearms were not permitted on the cell-house floor at Alcatraz, so Lageson carried the blackjack for protection.

Outside, the morning breeze was cool on his face. He could smell fresh-baked bread at a nearby bakery. Lageson caught the H Car. Fifteen minutes later, he reached the end of the line and walked down the long hill toward Pier Four.

He walked past the municipal pier, built during the Depression by the Works Progress Administration (WPA) as part of the San Francisco Maritime Recreational Area. The entire facility was appropriated by the Army during WWII and was now being redeveloped for civilian use. Fishermen were already using the pier, setting up their crab nets and smelt lines in the early morning hours. This morning, as always, when Lageson and the other Alcatraz guards collected at Pier Four, they were greeted by the friendly fishermen.

It was still a few minutes before the 6:55 boat from Alcatraz would dock. Ernie's thoughts turned to the unlikely chain of events that had brought him to San Francisco, Alcatraz, and his job as a prison guard.

Ernie certainly had never intended to become a prison guard. He was born and raised on the North Dakota prairie, the son of Norwegian immigrants. His parents valued education highly. Although Ernie wasn't a serious student, he received outstanding grades in high school and was urged by his instructors to go to college. He worked as a field hand on local farms during school vacations and borrowed extensively to finance his education at Concordia College, just across the state line in Moorhead, Minnesota. His parents wanted him to study medicine, but he instead chose education.

His first teaching job was in Kloten, a small farming community in east-central North Dakota. There he met and married Eunice McLean, a grade-school teacher. Ernie smiled as he thought of the pert, petite blonde and her lovely smile. *She's still pretty, even at thirty-seven.* During the next ten years, at a succession of jobs, Lageson the teacher became Lageson the superintendent in ever-increasingly large rural school districts in North Dakota. He was superintendent of the Clyde School District when the Great Depression finally made untenable trying to manage a school with dwindling resources and trying to manage his own life on the meager pay he and Eunice received for their efforts. At Clyde, Lageson not only ran the school district as superintendent but also taught several courses at the high school and coached the high-school basketball team. Eunice taught in the elementary grades, where their son Ernie was a student. Lageson even became somewhat of a community hero when he coached one of the finest high-school basketball teams in local history.

But the future for a young school superintendent was bleak in Depression-ravaged North Dakota. So Lageson investigated a federal civil-service job as an educational/custodial officer at Alcatraz Island Prison. The job description presented what seemed to him an outstanding challenge. He could work with some of America's most hardened criminals. He was captivated with the possibility of turning their lives around and returning even a few of his charges to society as productive citizens.

Of course, the job meant a move to California and a substantial increase in salary, too. The extra money would help him pay off the money he still owed for his college education after all these years. His friends, particularly those with whom he worked, argued against the move. Eunice and young Ernie, though, were in favor of it. California! The dream of every dust-bowl plains dweller. After all, if the job didn't work out, he could always go back to teaching, but this time in California instead of the dreary North Dakota plains.

Lageson took the job. He, Eunice, and young Ernie sold everything that wouldn't fit in a couple of suitcases and headed for San Francisco and Alcatraz Island.

Disillusionment set in early. Ernie found out that penology, at least as it was practiced at Alcatraz, was not what he expected. Although the work was interesting, the educational and rehabilitation programs at Alcatraz were almost nonexistent. Prisoners at Alcatraz were not trained or rehabilitated. They were simply warehoused. Ernie found himself to be nothing more than a prison guard, guarding men who were very nearly all beyond rehabilitation. True, many of the prisoners were highly intelligent, and Ernie enjoyed discussing intellectual and philosophical subjects with them. But the fact remained: Ernie was a prison guard, his duties primarily custodial.

Then World War II intervened. Although his job exempted him from military service, Ernie volunteered. He joined the Navy. But he was too old for officer-candidate school. Despite his degree, Ernie became an enlisted man. He found boot camp an enormous physical challenge but performed as well as the other trainees, many of whom were fifteen years younger. Both the officers and enlisted men called him "Pappy" Lageson. He became a physical education instructor for aviation cadets.

Ernie had a lot of time to think while he was away from his family and away from his job. He decided that he wanted to return to education. When he finally returned to Alcatraz, he checked the job market in the Bay Area and decided to go back to school to get his general secondary credential, which would allow him to become a California high-school principal. It would take two summer sessions of graduate work at the University of California at Berkeley, but he could use the GI Bill, so his tuition and books would be free. He and Eunice decided that he would leave Alcatraz in a year, attend both summer sessions, and return to teaching in the fall of 1947.

Ernie was confident and enthusastic about the future. His plan of action was clear. In the meantime, he would continue at Alcatraz, and do the best job he could. For now, his work day was about to begin. The 6:55 boat from Alcatraz was nearing Pier Four.

2

Most of the incoming passengers on the 6:55 launch from Alcatraz Island were working wives who lived in civilian quarters on the island but worked in the city, the wives of guards and other prison employees. The launch crew consisted of a boat operator and one prison guard. The guards were assigned this duty on a rotating basis. As the boat slid alongside the pier, boat officer Bob Sutter stepped ashore to secure it to the dock and helped the women passengers ashore.

Ernie and the other day-shift guards made up the entire passenger load to Alcatraz Island on the 6:55 return run. He and several of the other guards helped load the fresh milk, vegetables, and the morning newspapers that were ferried to the island each day. Ernie felt a soft spray of saltwater on his lips as Alcatraz Island loomed out of the morning fog.

Alcatraz Island was initially named Islos de los Alcatraces in 1775 by a Spanish Lieutenant, the first European to sail into San Francisco Bay. He named the barren rock for the large number of pelicans living there, *alcatraces* being the Spanish word for pelican. The Army first developed a fortification on the island in 1853; by the 1860s, the Army was housing military prisoners there.

Then, during Prohibition, federal law enforcement authorities decided the increase in crime called for an escape-proof penal facility to hold a new breed of criminal.

The newly-appointed director of the FBI, J. Edgar Hoover, was calling for aggressive measures to incarcerate such gangland characters as "Machine Gun Kelly," John Dillinger, "Baby Face" Nelson, and others who were cast in Robin Hood-like roles by the national press. Despite objections by Bay Area politicians who argued against construction of a "Devil's Island" in the middle of scenic San Francisco Bay, the Federal Bureau of Prisons swiftly moved forward with plans to develop Alcatraz into a maximum-security prison.

The island was an ideal prison site. It was situated one and a half miles from San Francisco, the nearest mainland point, and even further from Marin County and the East Bay. Because of the powerful tidal currents and chill water, only expert swimmers could swim from Alcatraz to the mainland. The steep, rocky shore of Alcatraz made it extremely difficult to operate a boat close to the island and nearly impossible to land a vessel on the beach.

Over the years, construction and development created three levels on the island. At water level on the north side of the island was the dock and freight-loading installation for the prison launch and larger boats carrying freight, passengers, or water. (The island had no natural water supply, so all fresh water was carried to the island in water tankers.) The powerhouse, which generated the island's electrical supply, was also at water level at the northwest end of the island.

The second level was residential. On the east end of the island were several single-family dwellings and a new apartment house. A duplex at the east edge of an old Army parade ground was occupied by Associate Warden E.J. Miller and his wife, and Captain Henry Weinhold and his family. The concrete parade ground was the only large, open space where children could play.

At the west end of the island on the two lower levels were two large buildings that housed the prison industries. There, between 100 and 125 inmates worked in various shops. The largest prison industry was the laundry, which washed thousands of tons of laundry annually for military and government installations in the Bay Area as well as for Alcatraz prisoners and residents. Prison uniforms and other government uniforms were produced in the clothing shop. Also among the industries were a tailor shop, shoe shop, furniture factory, and a mat shop that manufactured rubber mats for the decks of Navy and merchant marine vessels. There were also a machine shop, a dry-cleaning plant, and a cargo-net factory that produced cargo nets for government ships.

The third level of construction on the island, known to residents as "up top," contained the massive cell house, with its cells, kitchen, dining hall, hospital, administrative offices, and storage and support areas. Immediately adjacent to the west end of the cell house was the prison recreation yard, surrounded by a fifteen-foot wall and affording dramatic views of San Francisco, the Golden Gate Bridge, and Marin County. Also up top were the lighthouse, Coast Guard station, and the elegant homes of the warden and the prison doctor.

Scattered throughout the western two-thirds of the island were security towers, most of which were manned around the clock by trained and heavily armed officers. The most strategic of these towers was the Dock Tower, where the keys to the prison launch were kept when the boat was not in use. The entire dock and adjoining work area could be observed from this tower. The Road Tower was located immediately adjacent to the yard, connected to the top of the yard wall by a catwalk. The officer in this tower maintained the key to the yard-wall gate, through which the prisoners passed each day going to and from the work areas.

The Hill Tower stood west of the yard, overlooking the prison industry area. This tower was also connected by catwalks to the top of the yard wall. The officer on duty in the Hill Tower controlled movements through the gates to the work area.

There were also the Model Shop Tower, located

The Cell House

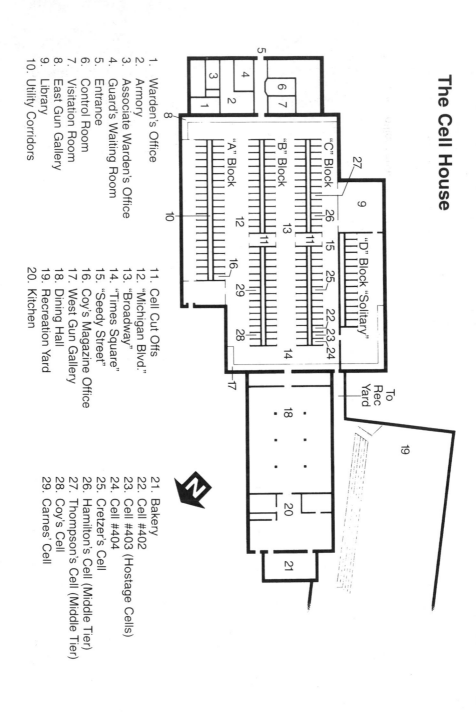

1. Warden's Office
2. Armory
3. Associate Warden's Office
4. Guard's Waiting Room
5. Entrance
6. Control Room
7. Visitation Room
8. East Gun Gallery
9. Library
10. Utility Corridors
11. Cell Cut Offs
12. "Michigan Blvd."
13. "Broadway"
14. "Times Square"
15. "Seedy Street"
16. Coy's Magazine Office
17. West Gun Gallery
18. Dining Hall
19. Recreation Yard
20. Kitchen
21. Bakery
22. Cell #402
23. Cell #403 (Hostage Cells)
24. Cell #404
25. Cretzer's Cell
26. Hamilton's Cell (Middle Tier)
27. Thompson's Cell (Middle Tier)
28. Coy's Cell
29. Carnes' Cell

Alcatraz Island Prison (1934 —1963)

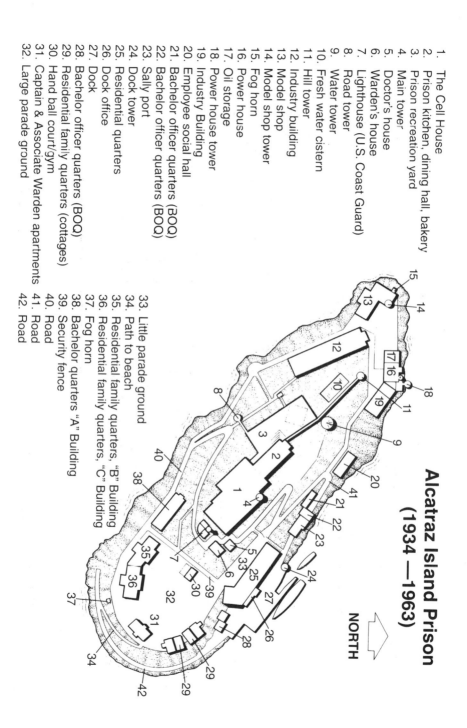

NORTH

1. The Cell House
2. Prison kitchen, dining hall, bakery
3. Prison recreation yard
4. Main tower
5. Doctor's house
6. Warden's house
7. Lighthouse (U.S. Coast Guard)
8. Road tower
9. Water tower
10. Fresh water cistern
11. Hill tower
12. Industry building
13. Model shop
14. Model shop tower
15. Fog horn
16. Power house
17. Oil storage
18. Power house tower
19. Industry Building
20. Employee social hall
21. Bachelor officer quarters (BOQ)
22. Bachelor officer quarters (BOQ)
23. Sally port
24. Dock tower
25. Residential quarters
26. Dock office
27. Dock
28. Bachelor officer quarters (BOQ)
29. Residential family quarters (cottages)
30. Hand ball court/gym
31. Captain & Associate Warden apartments
32. Large parade ground
33. Little parade ground
34. Path to beach
35. Residential family quarters, "B" Building
36. Residential family quarters, "C" Building
37. Fog horn
38. Bachelor quarters "A" Building
39. Security fence
40. Road
41. Road
42. Road

on top of one of the prison-industry buildings at the far west end of the island; a tower located near the powerhouse, also at the west end of the island; and the Main Tower, which was directly on top of the cell house. Individual guard houses were installed on top of the yard wall.

Each of the tower and yard-wall officers was armed with a Thompson submachine gun, a Springfield 30-06 rifle, and a .45-caliber automatic pistol.

The cell house was by far the largest building on the island. It was the heart of the prison. Ernie could see it now as the launch chugged closer to the island.

The ferry ride had taken ten minutes. The boatman maneuvered the launch around the southwest corner of Alcatraz and into its mooring slip. Ernie and the other prison guards walked up the ramp to the dock and through the metal detector at the dock office. The dock lieutenant noted each arrival in his card file. Since the prison launch was the only way on or off the island, by noting all departures and arrivals the prison administration could always know who was on the island.

From the dock, most of the guards boarded a small bus that carried them to the cell house. Ernie usually chose to walk. Unless it was raining, he climbed the steep paths and 300-odd stairs that led from the dock to the prison entrance.

"Just another way to keep in shape," he'd respond when the other officers chided him for turning down a ride. At thirty-seven, Ernie was in good shape, even better since returning from active Navy duty. He was five-feet, eight-inches tall and strode purposefully up the hill.

At the main entrance to the cell house, Ernie met Don Martin, his closest friend on the island. Martin and Lageson had trained together. The Martin family still lived on the island. Elnora Martin ran the small Alcatraz post office. Don Martin worked the morning watch from midnight till eight o'clock, but he was going home early today.

"They're still there, Ernie. Take care of them till I get back tonight," Martin called out.

"Yeah, I'm sure they're still here, and I hope they'll be here tonight, too," Ernie said, laughing along with Martin.

At 7:15 A.M. the guards gathered outside the front of the main prison entrance for the morning-officer roll call. Captain Henry Weinhold and the on-duty lieutenant stepped out in front of the assembled officers. "You may have heard the rumors that Bureau of Prisons Director Bennett is planning to visit Alcatraz soon," Weinhold said. "I've talked with the warden about it, and sure, there's always the chance that he'll visit, but there are no concrete plans for him to be here soon. You might pass that on to the inmates. We've had a lot of requests for interviews with the director."

"Yeah," somebody behind Ernie whispered,

"Probably 'Crazy Sam' Shockley complaining about us poisoning his food."

With roll call and announcements over, the officers headed for their duty stations. Ernie and the other cell-block officers entered the main cell house. Access to the cell house from the administrative offices was through the main gate, which was a full-time duty station for one officer. Operation of these doors and gates required action by not only the main-gate officer but also the armory officer. Located immediately adjacent to the main gate was the armory, the nerve center of the prison, which was manned at all times. The armory was constructed of steel walls, with thick, bulletproof glass and steel-bar windows containing gun ports. The sole entrance to the armory was through a single door, which locked and unlocked only from the inside. All firearms, weapons, and ammunition were stored in the armory.

Island communications were controlled from the armory switchboard, which had phone connections to every duty station on the island, all the residential and support areas, and the mainland. All weapons and ammunition maintained in the armory were individually signed in and out by the various officers manning stations requiring firearms.

To admit someone to the cell house through the main gate, the armory officer electrically retracted the shield over the lock on the outermost gate. The main gate officer then opened that gate from the inside with a key and allowed the person to pass through the first gate. That gate was then closed and locked and the shield moved back into place by the armory officer. The same procedure was repeated to open a second gate about ten feet away. Thereafter, two additional sliding gates, one barred and one solid, had to be opened to gain admittance to the cell-block area. Each of the four gates required a separate key. The final solid steel door had a bullet-proof viewing panel to permit the main gate officer to see into the cell house even with the door closed.

The main cell house contained three blocks of cells. Along the north wall was A Block, an outdated block of cells from the Army days, which had never been modernized. A Block did not house prisoners. It was instead used as a storage area. Next to A Block and in the center of the cell house was B Block. Along the south side of the huge room was C Block. All the prisoners in the island's general population were housed in either B Block or C Block. These each consisted of two rows of cells, back to back, three tiers high and 150 feet long. A utility corridor in which various utility lines were located ran down the length of each block behind the cells. Each block was divided into two sections by a ten-foot space referred to as "the cutoff," which made it possible to pass from one side to the other without having to go to the end of the building. On the main floor level, or "the flats," there were 28 cells on the west side of the cutoff, and 30 cells on the east side for a total of 58 cells on the lower level. Each of the two tiers above had a like number of cells, making a total of 174 per block with 84 total cells west of the cutoff and 90 on the eastern side.

Over the years, the convicts gave the corridors between the three blocks of cells names, which came to be accepted by everyone. The corridor between B Block and C Block down the center of the cell house was the widest of the three. It was known as Broadway. The corridor between A Block and B Block was Michigan Boulevard. The corridor on the south side of C Block was known as Seedy Street. This corridor ran between C Block and the isolation section of the prison, D Block. The west end of Broadway was referred to as Times Square, so named because a large clock was mounted on the west wall over the dining-hall entrance.

The upper tiers of B Block and C Block were reached by stairways at the ends of each block. Walkways along each upper tier projected out as overhangs over the floor-level cells.

In 1940, D Block was reconstructed to serve as a "prison within a prison." The south side of the building was remodeled to house isolation cells for the Alcatraz incorrigibles. D Block was separated from the main cell house by a soundproof wall with a single entry door at the west end. This door was kept locked at all times. The prisoners in D Block were either escape risks or risks to themselves, the institution, or other inmates. They were considered unfit for the general inmate population.

Across the east wall of the main cell house at the same height as the upper cell-block tiers was the east gun gallery. This was a narrow, barred catwalk with two levels connected at each end by ladders. Each level was approximately four feet wide and eight feet high. The lower level was approximately ten feet above the cell-house floor. The gallery was manned by an armed guard whenever all the prisoners were in the cell house. The only entry into the east gun gallery was through a door in the administrative section of the prison. There was no access from the gallery directly into the cell house.

Located along the west end of the cell house was the west gun gallery, which was manned at all times. This gallery projected into D Block along the west wall, then turned and ran along the south wall of D Block, a distance of approximately forty feet. In D Block, the gun gallery had three barred levels. The lower (floor) level was also enclosed in heavy wire mesh. Entry to the west gun gallery was through one outside door on the south side of the building. This door was reached from a catwalk that ran along the side of the building and could only be opened from the outside. When the west gun gallery officer came on duty, he was locked inside by the man he relieved and could only be released by his relief, again from outside the building. The entrance to the gallery was on the main-floor level of D Block. Just inside the south door was a ladder leading to the first tier of the gallery. A similar ladder connected the first tier to the second. Soundproof doors on both the first and second tiers permitted the officer on duty in the gallery to move back and forth between D Block and the main cell house.

There were also observation windows in the west gallery that looked down into the dining hall. If it became necessary, the gallery officer could fire into the dining hall through gun ports. He also controlled the operation of large canisters of tear gas mounted on the ceiling of the dining hall. The officer on duty in the gun gallery was armed with a rifle, an automatic pistol, and seventy-one rounds of ammunition. In addition to the firearms, there were tear-gas bombs, clubs, and gas masks stored in the gallery for use in the event of an uprising.

Each gallery was protected by a thirty-nine-inch-high sheet of steel covering the lower portion of each level that faced the cell house or D Block. Except for a toilet and a chair, the galleries contained no items of comfort.

At the west end of Broadway was the entrance to the dining hall. Entry was through two sliding gates, one barred and one solid. Beyond the dining hall was the kitchen and bakery, storage areas, and the kitchen steward's office. The dining hall contained twenty-two tables, each of which could accommodate ten inmates. Just inside and to the left of the dining-hall gate was a flight of stairs leading to the hospital. These stairs were guarded by locked doors at the bottom and the top. In addition to medical personnel, there was a guard on duty in the hospital at all times.

At the east end of Seedy Street was the prison library. Entry to the library was through a locked door from the cell house. There was no entry between the library and D Block. The only entrance to D Block was through the cell-house door at the west end of the building.

All significant cell-house keys were maintained in

the west gun gallery and were passed down on a rope to the officers in D Block or the cell house. Keys were immediately returned to the gallery after use. The keys opened the recreation-yard door, the D Block door, the dining-hall door, the basement door, and various other locks within the cell house. The standing order from the warden was that no door or gate was to be opened to permit or further an escape, even if the prisoners held hostages.

Ernie and the other guards walked briskly down Broadway to relieve the guards who had been on duty through the night. Ernie hadn't mentioned the tension he felt among the inmates to anyone except Eunice. He now wondered if it was just residual tension from the disturbance last week in D Block. Just a week before, on the night of April 25, a dozen convicts in the isolation block had started fires in their cells and destroyed property, protesting what they claimed was a lack of proper medical care for inmate Robert Stroud, who would later gain fame as "Birdman of Alcatraz." The uprising was quickly put down. Most of the custodial force considered it just a minor disturbance. Ernie hoped that's all it had been.

On the catwalk outside the west gun gallery, Officer Bert Burch, a craggy-faced veteran of many years of prison service, unlocked the doors and stepped into the lowest level of the west gun gallery in D Block. Burch had come to Alcatraz from Leavenworth in 1936. Short and slight, the native

Oklahoman was an intelligent man who spoke with a decided drawl. He, his wife, and son lived in the new apartment house, which was available only to the most senior officers. Burch exchanged pleasantries with the departing officer, who advised him that all was well in D Block. Burch went up the ladder to the second level and stepped to the front of the gallery. He glanced down at the main floor, where the morning-watch D Block officer was completing his last count before going off duty.

On the cell-house floor, Lieutenant Joseph Simpson and Captain Weinhold were marshaling the cellhouse custodial force for the 7:20 prisoner count. The wake-up bell sounded for the prisoners at 6:45 every morning. They had forty minutes to wash, dress, and prepare for the day's activities. Simpson was eager to get the count completed and effect the change of shift. He moved quickly to the west end of the cell house. At Times Square, he clapped his hands to get the attention of the custodial officers. "Okay, fellas, let's get the count and get them fed."

Simpson was a friendly, heavyset man, well liked by the other guards but feared and distrusted by many of the inmates. He was the leader of what the prisoners referred to as the "Goon Squad," the emergency response squad called to put down disturbances in the cell house with force. Simpson used a billy club if his demand for order was not obeyed immediately.

It was 7:30 A.M. Ernie and the other day-shift guards were all in place. It seemed like another routine day at Alcatraz.

3

Bernard "Bernie" Coy had slept fitfully, waking several times during the night as the hourly counts were taken and the cell-house officers walked by his cell. Now, as he lay on his bunk, he was excited and felt his heartbeat quicken as he thought of the upcoming events. He kept questioning himself, "Have I left anything out? Have I thought of everything? What could possibly go wrong? Can I count on all the guys to do the right thing?"

His concentration was broken by the voice of Lieutenant Joseph Simpson. "Good morning, Coy, how are you doing today?"

"Just fine, Mr. Simpson. Another day, another dollar."

Coy had been at Alcatraz nine years. Outwardly, he was cordial and good-natured. Even at forty-six, he was handsome, with steel-gray eyes and black hair. But despite his good looks and charm, he was a ruthless criminal. When he was sixteen, Coy had left home and joined the Army. He served with distinction for four years during World War I. In 1919 he reenlisted. Soon after he married, he deserted the Army and remained at large until he was arrested seven years later in Green Bay, Wisconsin, for burglary. He received two years in prison and a dishonorable discharge.

Bernie Coy was an accomplished painter and decorator, but he couldn't support himself and his wife during the Great Depression. He turned to armed robbery. He served three short prison terms for armed robbery over the next eleven years. Later, when he and the Stiles brothers robbed the bank in New Haven, Kentucky, they were caught almost immediately. Coy received a twenty-five-year sentence. When he was labeled an incorrigible at the federal prison at Atlanta, he was transferred to Alcatraz in 1937.

Coy's age alone brought him a certain amount of respect. His reputation as a fearless holdup man and an expert marksman with a rifle gave him a high standing in the prison social order.

Bernie Coy also had his share of enemies at Alcatraz. Many inmates disliked the way he showed respect for the guards and so carefully followed prison regulations. Others considered him eccentric because of his preoccupation with escape, which they considered only a fantasy. Other inmates thought he was smart enough to come up with an escape plan that would actually work.

The guards were also split in their reactions to Coy. Some guards saw Coy as nothing more than a shrewd convict waiting for an opportunity to escape, always planning, always conniving. But most of the guards considered him an intelligent, competent worker who carried out his assignments and stayed out of trouble. These guards appreciated the respect he showed for both the custodial force and the other inmates.

Coy became a model Alcatraz prisoner, perhaps having learned from his experiences in other prisons. He read extensively, primarily psychology and law books. He returned to painting and spent hours working with oils, painting beautiful views of the hills and valleys of western Kentucky from memory. He shared his talents with other inmates, too, teaching fundamentals to beginning artists and helping established artists improve their techniques. Coy also became an accomplished "cell-house lawyer," filing writs and briefs for himself and for other prisoners.

In November 1940, he filed a motion in the federal district court in Kentucky to vacate his sentence and correct what he argued was a violation of his right against double jeopardy. Officer Carl Sundstrom frequently helped inmates prepare writs and motions. Sundstrom thought the motion had some merit, even some precedents, in the federal courts. Coy and Sundstrom were especially optimistic when the court appointed a lawyer to handle Coy's appeal.

But after four years in the federal courts, Coy's appeal was denied. He had convinced himself that his appeal would get him off The Rock. Inside, he felt like a caged animal, though he continued to play the part of the perfect prisoner. With all hope now lost of being released by the courts, and sure he could not survive and remain sane until his sentence was served, Coy dedicated himself to the impossible—to escape from escape-proof Alcatraz.

He began to formulate a plan.

Coy decided that a successful break had to originate in the cell house, not from any of the work details, or even the recreation yard. So Coy asked for the choice assignment for his needs: library orderly. As library orderly, he distributed reading material from the library to the prisoners and moved freely throughout the main cell house. Coy was also allowed to take on an assignment as cell-house cleaning orderly. With these two jobs, he could observe procedures, study the habits of the guards and administrative officers, and work out the assignments and the schedules of the guards. In the morning, he carried out his duties as library orderly, making deliveries throughout the cell house and to D Block. In the afternoon, he worked at cleaning and polishing the floors and doing maintenance tasks assigned him by the cell-house officer. His work was always done promptly and efficiently. He never violated his privileges.

Coy enjoyed conversations with the officers, particularly the more educated ones. There were a number of former schoolteachers and administrators who, like Ernie Lageson, had come to Alcatraz during the Great Depression. Casual contact with the custodial force also gave Coy the opportunity to observe the guards' movements and habits. He memorized all the guards' strengths and, more importantly, their weaknesses. He studied their routines and kept careful notes.

There had been eight prison breaks since Coy came to Alcatraz in 1937, all of them unsuccessful. Coy had spent hours talking with the would-be escapees after they served their time in isolation and returned to the general population. He questioned the prisoners in detail to learn everything he could about their plans and why they had failed.

The first convicts to actually make it off the island were Ralph Roe and Ted Cole, who disappeared in 1937. They were never heard from again. It was commonly believed that both men perished in the treacherous waters of San Francisco Bay.

In 1941, John Bayless slipped silently away from the garbage detail one foggy day. The supervising guard was busy on the other side of the garbage truck when Bayless disappeared into the fog and made his way to the beach. He plunged into the water, but the frigid bay and swirling tide were too much for him. His body was battered against the rocks, and he was sick from having swallowed salt water. He was happy to be recaptured.

In 1943, four men—Floyd Hamilton, Fred Hunter, James Boreman, and Harold Brest—also made it into the bay. The bone-chilling water stopped that jailbreak, too. Hamilton and the others gained temporary freedom after they bound and gagged their shop foreman and Captain Weinhold. Even though they had covered themselves with heavy industrial grease and had flotation devices, the frigid water and swirling current were too much for them to overcome. Boreman was shot in the head by a volley of rifle fire as he treaded water waiting for the island launch to pick him up. Brest was picked up cold but unharmed. Hamilton and Hunter hid in caves. Hunter was captured the next day.

Hamilton avoided detection while in the water and was eventually given up for dead. A couple of guards erroneously reported seeing him disappear into the swift current running out to sea. In fact, he had dived under the surface of the water and swam back to a cave, where he hid for three days. Hamilton carried several bullet fragments in his left leg and ankle from police shoot-outs which, along with the current and cold water, prevented him from swimming away from the island.

Hamilton's three-day stay in the cave was an amazing feat. As the tide rose, twice a day, only a tiny pocket of air remained in the roof of the cave. He barely avoided drowning. Finally, nearly overcome by hypothermia and exhaustion, he returned to the industries area and was recaptured. Even though he had surrendered, Hamilton's three-day holdout only enhanced his already solid reputation with the other prisoners. From the stories of the inmates who had managed to make it to the water, Coy learned that the water was so cold that some level of hypothermia could be expected within thirty minutes. Hamilton had nearly died from exposure. The tide itself was so powerful that even strong swimmers were challenged by long swims in the bay. Even with homemade flotation equipment, Coy concluded that swimming from the island was not practical. He would need a boat, and the only boat he could count on being on the island was the island launch.

On a windy April morning in 1936, mentally disturbed inmate Joe Bowers was shot and killed while he was operating an incinerator located on the west side of the island. The official report showed that he was attempting to escape by climbing the fence, but the prisoners didn't believe it. The convicts decided that Bowers was chasing an errant piece of paper stuck to the top of the fence when an overly-aggressive tower guard opened fire.

The Bowers incident gave Coy the third element of his plan—the need to neutralize the tower guards during a breakout. Any successful breakout would have to be with guns blazing. Knives, after all, could be obtained from the kitchen or hand-fashioned from scraps of metal or plastic. But knives would only be effective against unarmed guards in face-to-face situations. Coy asked prisoner Charlie Livers to fabricate a gun out of wood. Convict Harry Mahoney, who worked in the woodworking shop, drilled holes in the wood. One of the convicts from the dock detail contributed shells pilfered from the Army laundry. Three .30-caliber and two .45-caliber bullets were surreptitiously collected from the pockets of soldiers' trousers sent to the island for cleaning. The convicts worked on the wooden gun for several months but never even tested it.

Coy also constructed a primitive flamethrower

with an internal plunger and a wooden handle from a heavy cardboard mailing tube. One end of the tube was sealed, except for a small hole. Coy tested the device with water and sprayed a small stream nearly thirty feet. He wanted to fill the tube with gasoline from the vehicle-maintenance area so he could injure and possibly incapacitate an officer from some distance away. The project stalled when he couldn't get gasoline or any other fuel for his flamethrower.

Since he had decided that the breakout would have to start inside the cell house, Coy also had to figure out how to get out of the cell house. Early afternoon seemed the best time for a break. From about 1:30 to 2:15 each day, one of the two cell-house officers was at lunch. During this forty-five-minute period, the work crews were back at work, and things were quiet in the cell house. One un-armed officer covered the entire cell house; his only backup was the armed guard in the west gun gallery. Occasionally, even the gallery officer was not there, since he also patrolled the D Block side of the gallery on the other side of a soundproof door.

Coy considered each of the several exits from the cell house. Every day the warden's inmate cooks passed through the main gate leading into the administrative offices at the east end of the cell house. They told Coy that storming this gate would be virtually impossible. The doors in the basement below the kitchen could only be opened from the outside, so Coy ruled out this gate, too. There was a door on the north end of the cell house, but Coy had never seen it used and had no idea if it even opened or where the keys might be kept.

The ventilator ducts and skylights in the ceiling were also a possibility. These could be reached with the large, rolling scaffold used to replace light bulbs in the ceiling. Escape through these openings would lead to the roof of the cell house, the site of the Main Tower. If the tower could be captured, the prize would be an automatic pistol, a rifle, and a Thompson submachine gun, along with perhaps two or three hundred rounds of ammunition. Since he would have to break through the skylight or vent to get to the Main Tower, the noise would alert the tower guard. Coy and his men would be easy targets.

Coy decided the most likely escape route from the cell house was the door to the recreation yard. This door was opened and closed dozens of times during the day. The key was kept in the gun gallery. Coy had seen this door opened and closed so many times he even knew the number of the key that controlled it. It was key 107. Once through the door and into the yard, the only barrier to freedom was the yard-wall gate, which led to the prison industries area. The key to the yard-wall gate was kept by the guard in the Road Tower.

Coy knew that the history of attacks by inmates against the manned towers was also less than encouraging. In April 1938 Whitey Franklin and his confederates, Jimmy Lucas and Tom Limerick, tried it. Limerick died instantly from a bullet between the eyes. Franklin was injured by two slugs from the tower guards' guns. Coy knew that if any Alcatraz tower was to be taken, the attackers had to be armed and ready to return the fire of the tower officer.

The final element of Coy's plan was the need to take hostages. Although prison policy forbade opening any cell-house door during an escape attempt, even under threat of death to a hostage, Coy believed the guards would give in rather than be responsible for the death of a fellow officer. Hostages could also be used as shields, not allowing the guards clear shots at the escaping inmates. They might also be used to trade for weapons or the boat key, and would undoubtedly prove just as valuable when the escapees reached the mainland.

The custodial force was the most obvious source of hostages, but there were dozens of wives and preschool children on the island, separated from the cell house and prison-industry locations by nothing more than a cyclone fence topped by four strands of barbed wire. The civilian residences on the east and south sides of the island were not protected by guard towers. Only Building 64—a civilian barracks—was protected by the guard in the Dock Tower on the north side of the building. The tower platform was at the same level as the outside upper balcony of Building 64, which overlooked the dock. Coy believed that if he had women and children hostages on this balcony, the Dock Tower officer would be forced to release not only the boat key but his weapons as well.

Unfortunately, the cell-block guards did not carry guns. The only guns in the cell-block building were in the west gun gallery. The west gun gallery held guns, ammunition, and the key to the yard door. If only he could somehow take the west gun gallery. Coy had his plan. Now he just needed to figure out how to implement it.

Coy rejected the idea of cutting through the bars of the west gun gallery. That had been tried by a group of D Block inmates in 1939. "Doc" Barker, Rufus McCain, William Martin, Dale Stamphill, and Henri Young broke out of D Block by cutting the bars on their cells and the bars covering the windows. They made it to the beach before they were captured. Coy knew that the cell-house bars, including the bars protecting the west gun gallery guard, had since been upgraded with a new, toolproof design. These new bars had kept Joe Cretzer, Arnold Kyle, Sam Shockley, and Lloyd Barkdoll from cutting their way out of the mat shop in 1941.

Early one morning, as he pushed his cart of magazines and library materials along Broadway and studied the details of the west gun gallery, Coy made a crucial observation. He couldn't believe he had never noticed it before. He quickly pushed his cart down the broad corridor to a point immediately below the gun gallery and stared up into the bar structure of the top tier. The gallery bars were about five inches apart and were sunk into the floor of the lower tier of the gallery. From there they rose to about seven feet above the floor of the upper tier of the gallery, then curved at a gentle angle and were imbedded in the west wall of the cell house. Horizontal cross-members were installed at approximately eighteen-inch intervals to strengthen the vertical bars. This created a series of openings between the bars eighteen inches high and five inches wide. At the top of the gallery where the bars curved, there were no cross-members. It was not reinforced.

Coy knew that the curved area of each bar would be its weakest point. I've found it. Son of a bitch, I've found it, he thought. He stood staring into the upper reaches of the west end of the cell house. If he could somehow spread the bars far enough for him to squeeze through into the top tier, he was on his way!

4

Now that Coy had discovered a way to reach the gun gallery, he began detailing his plan. It was one thing to know that the bars could probably be spread enough for a small person to squeeze through. It was quite another to figure out how to spread those bars and, just as important, when to attack the gun gallery.

Coy continued to study the habits and idiosyncrasies of all the cell-house officers on the day watch. Since the outline of his plan was complete, he could now focus on the guards who might be on duty during the break, looking for weaknesses in routine or personality. He also carefully noted how often during the day the prison administrators visited the cell house, noting the times and lengths of their visits. He paid particular attention to the habits of

Bert Burch, who worked as the day-watch officer in the west gun gallery.

Coy noted that between one and two o'clock, Burch spent most of his time on the D Block side of the gallery. From inmates who had served time in D Block, he learned that the officer lounged in the midday sun and either dozed or read during this quiet, early afternoon period. To encourage this habit, Coy saw to it that Burch always had a supply of the most desirable reading material from the library. He passed copies of such popular magazines as *Look*, *Life*, and *Colliers* up to Burch as soon as they were received and before any of them were distributed to the inmates.

Because of his excellent job performance, Coy was now trusted to work with little supervision. He made a habit of frequently working out of sight of the officers but always with a ready explanation of where he was and what he was doing. He used this unsupervised time to gather more information.

Coy needed to measure the distance between the gallery bars so he would know how much he would need to spread them to allow him to slip through. He also had to measure his own body. Using his artists' materials, he fashioned crude but reasonably accurate devices to measure the dimensions of his head, chest, shoulders, hips, and thighs. He was concerned that his abnormally large ears would present a problem when he tried to get his head through the narrow space. During one of his brief absences from the cell-house officer's view, Coy scrambled up the south wall of the cell house and measured the space between the bars of the east gun gallery. He assumed that the two galleries would be identical. He was able to measure the bars at the east end with relative ease when the gallery was unoccupied. Later he was lucky enough to find an inmate painter working near the west gallery who was willing to measure the bars on the west gallery. As he predicted, the space between the bars in both galleries was nearly the same, ranging from five to five and one-half inches.

After careful measurement, Coy was satisfied that his thin frame, lubricated with industrial grease, would fit through an opening seven inches wide. This meant he had to spread the two bars by about two inches. There would be no opportunity to practice. He knew that his planning had to be precise or he could end up squeezed between the bars. Caught. Squealing like a fucking pig waiting for slaughter, he thought, and quickly rejected the image.

Later, Coy decided that the break would begin while the cell-house officer was shaking one of Coy's confederates down as he passed from the kitchen to his cell. It was vital that the gun-gallery officer be on the D Block side for at least ten to fifteen minutes during this time so Coy could attack the cell-house officer and the two inmates could overpower him and tie him up.

Gallery officer Burch's habits were totally predictable. By 1:30 every afternoon, he was seated on his stool on the D Block side of the gallery. Coy planned to attack and overpower Burch when he returned to the cell-house side of the gallery so as not to alert the D Block officer, who would certainly sound the alarm if he knew what was going on.

If Coy could get Burch's guns, he could invade D Block and would then control the entire cell house. With key 107, he and the others could exit through the cell-house door into the yard, taking the cell-house officers and the guard on duty in the yard as hostages. Coy planned to kill the officers stationed in the Road Tower and on the yard wall using Burch's rifle. Using the ladder from the kitchen, he would scale the wall, get more guns from the yard-wall sentry box and the Road Tower, and get the key to the yard-wall gate. From there it would be an easy trip to the apartment houses and the civilian hostages.

Coy's group would have three automatic pistols, three rifles, and two Thompson submachine guns, along with hundreds of rounds of ammunition. If they were able to take the Hill Tower, they would have another pistol, rifle, and machine gun. Three more guns would be taken from the Dock Tower along with the boat keys. The inmates could then commandeer the launch and make their way to Marin County with as many hostages as they chose to take.

Two problems remained. First, Coy had to pick the men to be on his team. Second, he needed to design, fabricate, and smuggle the bar spreader into the cell house.

Coy immediately settled on the four men he wanted as part of his team. First, there was Rufus "Whitey" Franklin, a quiet Alabaman with a high-pitched voice and slow southern drawl. Franklin was serving a life sentence in Alabama for murder when he was given a thirty-day parole to attend his mother's funeral. During this humanitarian leave, he robbed a national bank and was sentenced to thirty years in federal prison.

Franklin was transferred to Alcatraz in 1936. Within three years, he was part of a bloody escape attempt that resulted in the beating death of guard Royal Cline. Franklin and two accomplices in the furniture shop overpowered Cline and beat him to death with hammers, then slipped through an un-barred window on the third floor of the industries building, scrambled to the roof, and tried to attack guard Harold Stites in the Model Shop Tower. They beat on the glass walls of the tower with hammers and pieces of scrap steel, but the tower's glass walls were shatterproof. The tower's glass walls weren't bulletproof, however. Stites blazed away at Franklin and the other inmates first with his pistol, then with his rifle, killing one man instantly and seriously wounding Franklin.

Unfortunately, Franklin was still confined in D Block and could not be privy to any of Coy's planning. Coy needed Franklin's expertise with locks but needed more the desperate fearlessness that Franklin had shown in his own escape attempt. Coy planned to take control of the cell house and D Block, so

Franklin could be released once the escape was underway.

Second on Coy's short list was Joe Cretzer. Like Franklin, he was fearless and had attempted escapes from both McNeil Island and Alcatraz. Cretzer was experienced with firearms. He also knew the San Francisco Bay Area well. He had underworld contacts in the Bay Area, and Coy knew they would need help once they made it to the mainland. Cretzer's criminal background was impressive. Along with Arnold Kyle, he had headed one of the most violent bank robbery gangs on the West Coast. His exploits earned him the fifth ranking on the list of America's Ten Most Wanted Criminals, an accomplishment of which he was very proud. Cretzer had also been confined to D Block since his abortive escape attempt in 1941 from the mat shop. Cretzer, in fact, was in an isolation cell, totally out of the mainstream of prison life. But he, too, would be available once Coy took over D Block.

Then, early in 1946, Joe Cretzer was released from isolation after a stay of nearly five years. Following standard procedures, he was initially placed on idle status pending a permanent work assignment. Cretzer was given a cell on the flats of C Block, across from the library.

Short and stocky, just five-feet, six-inches tall and weighing only 145 pounds, Cretzer was a handsome man, with a nearly angelic face set off by brown, piercing eyes and jet-black, wavy hair. During his criminal career, he had prided himself on his stylish dress. His drab prison uniform constantly irritated him. In his heyday as one of the top bank robbers in America, he was always flawlessly groomed and presented a nearly theatrical appearance in suit, tie, and snap-brimmed hat. Coy immediately felt drawn to Cretzer. They spent months talking together, refining Coy's plan.

Coy thought it important to consult Floyd Hamilton about the breakout. Hamilton, after all, had been Number One on the FBI's Most Wanted List. He had been one of the chief lieutenants in the famous Bonnie Parker and Clyde Barrow gang. Hamilton, too, was familiar with firearms and had attempted to escape from Alcatraz. Unfortunately, Hamilton had a bad leg from bullet wounds he received during a shoot-out with the FBI. Coy decided to keep Hamilton informed but to not rely on him.

Thirty-eight-year-old Hamilton was one of the toughest and most famous inmates on Alcatraz. He and his brother Ray grew up with Parker and Barrow in Dallas, Texas. The four were lifelong friends and criminal partners until the bloody shoot-out deaths of Bonnie and Clyde and the electrocution of Ray. Hamilton was the sole survivor of that famous gang. When he was captured, Hamilton boasted, "They got me in jail now, all right, but they ain't gonna keep me there. They don't make jails that strong." Hamilton was convicted of several counts of armed robbery and was transferred to Alcatraz almost immediately after sentencing.

When Coy mentioned the escape to Edgar Cook, his coworker in the library, Cook was quick with an answer. "Sure, count me in," he said. But he had only been on Alcatraz for about a month when Coy first approached him in the summer of 1945. Coy and Cook discussed the plan in detail over the next several weeks, but Coy never told Cook the names of the other inmates who would be involved, and Cook didn't know Coy well enough to trust his judgment. Cook began to have second thoughts about participating but never shared his reservations with Coy. Coy was counting on him.

Marv Hubbard also fit the profile Coy was looking for. He was thoroughly familiar with firearms. He had considerable experience with automatic weapons, including submachine guns. He had been involved in a number of shoot-outs and several times had fought his way out of police ambushes. He had escaped from jails throughout the South, fighting on even when outnumbered and outgunned. Once when he and his partner were trapped in a roadblock in a narrow canyon with police surrounding him, he fought ferociously until he was so badly wounded he could no longer fire back.

Hubbard was thirty-three and a muscular man, somewhat stocky at five feet, seven inches and 155 pounds. He was powerful but not agile, having never cared much for athletic activity. His rimless wire glasses gave him a studious appearance, and, although he read a good deal, he was not particularly intelligent. His reading tastes ran generally to fiction and action stories. Hubbard was soft-spoken and rarely raised his voice, even when he was angry. Although he was friendly with Coy, he mostly kept to himself.

Born to Alabama sharecroppers, Hubbard had left school as soon as he was old enough to work the fields. As a result, he didn't learn to read or write until he was in prison. He worked as a bricklayer, but the Great Depression brought hard times to the building industry. Not only did he have trouble finding work as a bricklayer, like most men during the Depression, he had trouble finding any work at all. Unable to support his family, Hubbard turned to crime and became an armed robber while he was still a teenager. He was arrested several times by local police and served several short jail terms, escaping three times.

On August 7, 1942, Hubbard was serving a short term in the Walker County Jail in Jasper, Alabama. He and two others overpowered the jailer and escaped. Over the next several days, they stole several vehicles, sometimes kidnapping the owners, as they proceeded east through north-central Alabama.

They were eventually captured following a spectacular gun battle by a 200-man posse of FBI agents, state troopers, local police, and outraged private citizens. Hubbard later charged that he was beaten by the FBI, forced to sign a false confession, then coerced into waiving his right to a lawyer and coerced into pleading guilty. He was initially imprisoned at Atlanta but was transferred to The Rock in November 1944.

Hubbard's habeas corpus petition was still working its way through the courts. His attorney assured him it stood an excellent chance to succeed, but he readily joined Coy's group anyway. "I'm with you,

Bernie," he repeatedly assured Coy. "I'd rather take my chances with you and a gun on Alcatraz than with the fucking, crooked courts in Tennessee."

Since the plan involved taking the prison launch, Coy seriously considered bringing Blackie Audett into the venture because of his knowledge of boats and experience as a boat operator. Audett had worked in the Puget Sound fishing fleet. Unfortunately, he and Audett did not get along well, so Coy had Joe Cretzer approach Audett. He rejected the offer. "No, Joe, I'm a short-timer. I can't risk it. I'll be off this fucking rock pile in less than a year, so trying to bust out don't make no sense. But thanks for the offer."

Coy also thought about including Cretzer's brother-in-law Kyle. He had the necessary background and credentials, and the two men got along well. Coy decided against including Kyle, however, thinking that he wanted Cretzer along but didn't want Cretzer in control. Coy thought Cretzer was headstrong and reckless and was sure that under pressure his decision making would become rash and emotional. Cretzer was a tough man but too unpredictable to be a good leader. Coy worried that if he and Cretzer had a disagreement during the break, Cretzer and Kyle might try to take over. Coy wanted absolute and unchallenged control. Luckily, Cretzer never pushed for his brother-in-law to be included.

Coy knew he would also need a gofer, somebody who would back him up and follow orders without question. He chose a young Oklahoma Indian, Clarence Carnes, also known to his friends as Joe. Coy liked the youngster and felt sorry for him. Carnes was only eighteen years old. He faced the real possibility of spending the rest of his life in prison, and, given his record, much or all of it on Alcatraz. The boy was strong and, by reputation, a tough fighter. Coy believed he would follow orders with dedicated loyalty and could be counted on if things got rough. Carnes's cell was directly across the corridor from his library office, so Coy spent a lot of time getting to know the young man. Carnes obviously admired Coy and would surely support Coy if a dispute arose within the group. Coy knew that in a dispute both Carnes and Hubbard would favor him over Cretzer.

On July 6, 1945, when he arrived on Alcatraz, Joe Carnes was the youngest inmate ever to serve time on the island. A full-blooded Choctaw Indian, Carnes was a quiet youngster who kept to himself. He was withdrawn, introverted, and had few good friends. He had now been at Alcatraz nearly ten months but had not received a regular work assignment. He had requested assignment to the kitchen. The request was under consideration. Since no kitchen openings were currently available, rather than take other employment, he continued in idle status.

Carnes spent much of his time maintaining his excellent physical condition. He exercised regularly in his cell and was proud of his strong, muscular body. He was learning chess and played regularly during recreation periods in the yard. He had also

developed his friendship with Coy, who was beginning to interest the young inmate in reading.

When he was only sixteen, Carnes and another
boy held up a service station in Atoka, Oklahoma,
not far from the reservation where they lived. The
twenty-two-year-old attendant was both amused and
angered by the robbery attempt. He threw a pop
bottle at Carnes and ordered him out of the station,
totally ignoring the pistol Carnes held in his hand. In
a flash of anger at not being taken seriously, Carnes
killed the young man. The two would-be robbers ran
from the station without ever touching the cash
drawer. After pleading guilty in an Oklahoma state
court, Carnes received a life sentence. In 1945, he
and two others escaped from Granite State Reformatory, stealing a truck and kidnapping the owner. For
this he received ninety-nine years in federal court
under the Lindbergh Act.

Coy also needed help from other inmates who,
while not joining the breakout, might help with the
details. Someone who worked in the prison machine
shop would have to make whatever Coy used to
spread the bars of the gun gallery. It could then be
smuggled piece by piece into the kitchen and then
into the cell house, where it would be stored until
Coy used it to break into the gallery. The maker of
the bar spreader and the smugglers to move it into
the cell house would have to be recruited and paid,
somehow. Since Hubbard worked on the dining-hall
food line, he had access to extra food, particularly

desserts, which could be served to Coy's helpers. Food and even home brew could be smuggled out of the kitchen, too, for payoffs.

To bring the bar spreader from the machine shop to the cell block, would require someone with a job like Coy's that allowed him to move around fairly freely. Ed Mrozik was the inmate plumber. Mrozik was a Minneapolis bank and post-office burglar whose gang had been dubbed by the press as the "Cream Can Bandits" because they carried their burglary tools in large metal cream cans. Mrozik had been dedicated to the "easy life" of burning and drilling his way to riches from bank vaults, but he had also worked as a plumber long enough to attain journeyman status. When he was transferred from Leavenworth to Alcatraz, he spent his first two years in isolation for refusing to work when his request for employment in the kitchen was denied. Coy knew Mrozik would be susceptible to a food bribe.

As the indoor plumber, Mrozik moved freely between the kitchen and the C Block utility corridor where the plumbing supplies and tools were stored. Since the kitchen was an ongoing source of plumbing problems anyway, Hubbard could always create a situation requiring a plumber. Mrozik could smuggle the bar spreader, a piece at a time, from the kitchen into the utility corridor, where it could be hidden until Coy needed it. Mrozik agreed to do it. "But not just extra desserts," he said, "extra everything. I've got a huge appetite."

Coy also thought he might need some help in D Block. Louie Fleish was one of the D Block orderlies.

Although Coy thought he would not be interested in joining the escape because of the violence and gunplay that was likely, Fleish was known as a "standup con." Coy thought Fleish would help, if needed, in D Block.

Another inmate who wanted in on the breakout was Buddy Thompson. He was twenty-nine and had been on Alcatraz less than six months. He was a handsome man, slightly stocky yet well built with hazel eyes and chestnut-brown hair. He had a hard face, and his close-set eyes gave him a Eurasian appearance. He rarely smiled. In fact, he usually looked angry. He arrived in November 1945 and was quickly absorbed into one of the Alcatraz cliques. A Texan, Thompson was accepted by the "redneck society," a group of Southerners who considered themselves superior to the other inmates. They tended to band together during recreation periods and often sought the same work assignments. They also were always ready to defend each other in fights, carried grudges for one another, and willingly performed acts of revenge on behalf of one of their number against outsiders. Being a cop killer gave Thompson a solid reputation.

Thompson left home as a teenager, saying he wanted to be on his own and learn a trade, but by age fifteen he was in reform school as an armed robber. Throughout the 1930s he drifted from town to town throughout Mississippi and Alabama pulling holdups of stores, bars, and service stations. By 1944, his reputation was such that he was an immediate suspect in any armed robbery committed in

Alabama or Mississippi, so he shifted his base of operations to Amarillo, Texas.

On March 12, 1945, he and a friend were arrested by Lem Savage, an Amarillo police detective. Savage handled the daylight arrest by himself, did not call for backup, and, after only a perfunctory search, placed the two prisoners in the front seat of his unmarked police car without handcuffs. Thompson drew a small revolver from his sock and began shooting. The gun fired five times, killing Savage and wounding Thompson and his friend. The fugitives commandeered a vehicle, kidnapped the occupants, and headed west on Route 66. They were captured within hours by the FBI. Thompson ultimately received a ninety-nine-year sentence in federal court for kidnapping and a life sentence in a Texas state court for murder. He was first sent to Leavenworth but, given the length of his sentences, was transferred almost immediately to Alcatraz.

Coy also knew that many other inmates would want to join in the break, especially if he succeeded in getting the gun-gallery weapons and breaking out of the cell house and then the yard. Coy hadn't decided quite what to do if somebody like "Crazy Sam" Shockley disrupted his carefully orchestrated plan.

Shockley had been on Alcatraz since September 1938, nearly eight years. Five of those years were spent in isolation, totally cut off from the outside world. Crazy Sam was a mentally retarded, paranoid schizophrenic.

Born in Oklahoma and raised in rural poverty,

Shockley left school to work on the family farm at the age of twelve. Within a year he began to exhibit signs of instability and twice attempted to run away from home. During his teen years, his personality disorders became more pronounced. He left home for good at eighteen and embarked on a career as a petty criminal. A year later, while serving time in the state reformatory, he was severely beaten by another prisoner and suffered a serious head injury. A year later he suffered a second brutal beating, this one with a nightstick, and received further major head trauma.

For the next five years, he drifted aimlessly throughout rural parts of the South doing odd jobs and committing petty crimes. Shockley's life of crime peaked and ended on March 15, 1938, when he and a confederate robbed a bank in the Oklahoma village of Paoli and kidnapped the bank president and his wife. Following a guilty plea, Shockley received a life sentence for his part in the robbery and subsequent kidnapping.

His initial incarceration was at Leavenworth, where testing disclosed he had an IQ of sixty-eight, equivalent to a mental age of ten years, ten months. Prison medical personnel also confirmed episodes of hallucination and serious emotional instability. Although the Leavenworth authorities were unsure of a diagnosis, they knew Shockley was unpredictable, irrational, and potentially violent, as well as emotionally and mentally deranged. He was incapable of coping with the normal prison environment, presenting a significant risk to himself and others. Rather than place him in the Medical Center for Federal Prisoners at Springfield, Missouri, however, which was equipped to deal with such cases, the authorities sent Shockley to Alcatraz. Forty-two percent of the patients at Springfield were diagnosed schizophrenics and were receiving treatment. For some reason, Sam Shockley was not among them.

From the day he arrived at Alcatraz, Shockley's psychiatric symptoms and his conduct made him a problem for the custodial force. During his initial indoctrination period, they found that his intelligence-test scores were lower than those recorded only a few months earlier at Leavenworth. His mental condition was deteriorating.

Throughout the early 1940s at Alcatraz, Shockley's condition continued to deteriorate. He displayed classic schizophrenic symptoms, including paranoia, hallucinations, disorientation, and auditory delusions. In 1942, the prison physician, Dr. Romnay M. Ritchey, reported Shockley was "emotionally very unstable with episodes of hallucination. His conduct has been erratic and unpredictable. He would likely break down again under the confusion and tension of a disaster and be dangerous to those about him. His transfer is suggested on that ground." He was not transferred. When he refused to work anywhere but in the kitchen, he was placed in isolation, where he remained for the rest of his stay on Alcatraz.

Shockley was unstable, but he could be included in the breakout. In fact, Coy had decided he would allow anybody to come along if they stayed out of the way. There could be strength in numbers, particularly if they could get more guns from the towers. There would be plenty of room on the boat. More inmates loose on the mainland would provide greater distraction for the police. Coy was determined to keep the number of active participants small, but he was willing to accept a mass breakout if it worked out that way.

5

Designing the bar spreader was easy for someone who had grown up with Model As and Model Ts. All Coy needed was a simple screw jack consisting of a nut, bolt, and sleeve. Turning the nut would drive the bolt and sleeve in opposite directions, forcing the bars apart. Using a pair of pliers to turn the nut on the well-lubricated bolt would develop tremendous power. Coy had a friend in the machine shop who owed him a favor. For a few extra desserts supplied by Hubbard, the inmate would probably agree to construct the bar spreader. The plumber, Mrozik, would supply the long-handled pliers, which could be stored along with the spreader.

The large parts of the bar spreader could be smuggled into the kitchen by means of a long-established smuggling system, a garbage can with a false bottom. The false bottom had been constructed of wooden slats from produce boxes cut and shaped to fit over the actual bottom of the can. The pieces of wood were precisely cut, fitted into place, and tightly wedged together, creating a compartment about two inches deep. The fit and color of the fake bottom was so similar to the interior of the can that it wasn't noticeable. It had been passed over by even the most careful guards.

The easiest place for the bolt, nut, and sleeve to be placed into this container was at the garbage disposal site. Garbage was regularly collected from around the island, including the cell house, the prison kitchen, the civilian residential areas, and the prison industries. The garbage cans were placed in the back of a pickup truck and hauled to an open chute on the southwestern cliffs of the island, where the garbage was dumped and carried by gravity into the bay.

If the parts could somehow be moved from the machine shop to the garbage disposal area, they could be inserted into the special can and delivered to the kitchen. Getting the bar spreader into the cell house really became a group project.

The fabricated spreader parts could first be hidden in a toilet that the machine shop shared with the prison laundry. Floyd Hamilton and Jay Lynch, both Coy's friends, worked in the laundry. They could retrieve the parts and hide them in the laundry. There was a constant flow of clean and dirty laundry between the laundry and the dock. The laundry was carried back and forth by one of the prison's pickup trucks. The parts could be greased and wrapped with tape to protect them from the salty, damp air and could be hidden in the laundry pickup.

At the end of the day, all the island vehicles, including the laundry and garbage trucks, were parked in a storage area on the dock. With the two pickups parked near one another, the small package could be plucked from its hiding place on the laundry truck and hidden in the garbage truck, where eventually it could be taken to the dump and transferred to the false-bottomed kitchen garbage can.

Plumber Ed Mrozik now became a key player in Coy's plan. Mrozik would smuggle the bar spreader from the kitchen, where Marv Hubbard would create some work needing a plumber, to the cell block, in his box of tools and parts. A nut, bolt, and sleeve wouldn't stand out among his tools. Any other method of smuggling the spreader parts into the cell block would have to take into account the metal detector that all the inmates had to pass through, except those few prisoners who had metal plates or shrapnel in their bodies. These inmates were always in demand to smuggle bits of metal into the cell block.

Mrozik could also put industrial grease with the spreader parts so it would be available during the escape. The grease could be carried into the cell house from the work area by another of Coy's friends and slipped to Mrozik during a weekend recreation period in the yard. The grease would lubricate the nut and bolt for ease of operation and would also be smeared on Coy's upper body and hips to help him squeeze through the bars.

Buddy Thompson worked in the tailor shop and agreed to make Coy a sturdy cloth drawstring bag to hold the assembled spreader, long-handled pliers, and pouch of grease. The drawstring would permit the bag to be tightly closed to protect the contents and would be long enough to allow Coy to hang the bag around his arm or neck as he scrambled up the bars of the gun gallery.

Coy and his confederates had all the time in the world. Coy stressed to everybody that precision was far more important than speed. Coy took a lot of time and spent a lot of effort educating the inmates who would handle the parts as to the precise times the pieces would be moved. Coy warned those who were assisting him, "We're here for twenty-five years, Old Man, so we've got plenty of time to do it right. Don't fuck things up by going too fast and being sloppy. We want to be sure we get this stuff into the cell house." It took weeks to construct the bolt and sleeve, and just as long to move the parts into the cell house.

The payoffs to the participants, in addition to special food handling arranged by Hubbard and his friends in the kitchen, would include special treatment by Coy in the distribution of magazines and library materials, extra cigarettes rolled by Coy and his companions, and occasional nips of home brew prepared and smuggled out of the kitchen by Hubbard and others. It was a long, deliberate process. But Coy was convinced it would work.

6

By late April 1946, after years of planning and preparation, everything was ready. Coy had been dieting for months, melting his already trim frame from 165 pounds to 140. He was sure he was now slim enough to pass easily through a seven-by-fifteen-inch opening. For more than a year he had been exercising and strengthening his arms and upper body until, despite his forty-six years, he believed he had greater upper body strength than at any other time in his life. The spreader, grease, and pliers were all in place. With the possible exception of Whitey Franklin, the participants were ready to go. Franklin was still in isolation and, for all Coy knew, might even be in solitary. The break would go with or without him.

Two factors convinced Coy that the time was right to execute his plan. First was the assignment of

Officer Cecil Corwin as the officer in charge of D
Block. Coy learned while eavesdropping that May 2
would be Corwin's first day back from a two-week
vacation and that he was scheduled to start as the D
Block officer on the day watch. In his mid-fifties,
Corwin was one of the least aggressive officers on
the staff. While he was a decent man who treated the
inmates fairly and respectfully, Coy viewed Corwin
as indecisive and spineless, one of the best officers
he could hope for in the sensitive and highly influ-
ential role of D Block officer. Even if Corwin were
to hear the attack on Burch, Coy gambled that his
indecision and fear would keep him from turning on
the alarm.

Second, Officer Ernie Lageson, recently back
from wartime service in the Navy, was serving as
officer in charge of the cell house with William Miller
as his assistant. While Lageson normally took his
lunch early, Miller had requested the early lunch.
Lageson had agreed. As a result, Lageson ate between 1:30 and 2:00 and always left the cell house
to eat in the administration offices. That was the
same time Bert Burch, the west gun-gallery officer,
took his afternoon break, out of sight of the cell
block. Perfect!

Discussing the plan with Cretzer, Coy explained
why he didn't want Lageson involved in any of the
escape activity. "You know that when Lageson goes
to lunch, Miller is alone on the floor. Lageson is a
tough little bastard. I'd rather not have to deal with
him," Coy explained. "There's no way he's going to
let me get behind him when he's shaking Hubbard

down. And we can't risk taking him on face to face. He carries a blackjack, and he'd probably club the shit out of us before we could take him down. He also knows judo, and he's in really good shape from the Navy. He's just too much of a risk. We need him out of the cell house."

The decision was made. The break would go on Thursday, May 2, as soon as Lageson left for lunch. "That gives us plenty of time," Coy explained to Cretzer. "We've got to be out and down on the dock before the 3:25 boat leaves. That gives us almost two hours to get out of the cell house, which should be plenty of time." The word was passed. The countdown began.

As the cell-house officers prepared for the morning count, the day-watch tower guards assumed their posts. Jim Comerford walked up the stairway to the top of the Dock Tower and locked the trapdoor in the tower floor. Comerford was a big man with a wild shock of hair surrounding his friendly face. He held a masters degree in English, and, like a number of the officers, Alcatraz was his first job in the penal service. Immediately upon assuming his post, Commerford propped his Thompson submachine gun against the interior glass wall of the tower and lowered the boat key to the operator waiting below. The next boat to San Francisco was the 8:10, which would transport the nonresident morning-watch officers and carry the first wave of schoolchildren to San Francisco.

In the Hill Tower, Elmus Besk gazed pensively out at the calm water of the bay. At the Road Tower, Irv Levinson huffed and puffed his way to the top of the stairs. A happy-go-lucky bachelor, Levinson was a heavyset, friendly man, well liked by all. As each tower officer assumed his post, he reported by phone to the armory officer, Cliff Fish.

In the kitchen things were running at a hectic pace. It was less than ten minutes until breakfast. Food was being wheeled into the dining hall on carts and loaded onto the steam tables. Chief Steward Robert Bristow was in charge of the convict kitchen detail of twenty-three inmates who worked under the custodial supervision of officers Larry O'Brien and Joe Burdett. In addition to monitoring the kitchen activity, O'Brien and Burdett took the morning count and passed it on to cell-house officer Lageson.

"All twenty-three accounted for, Ernie," Burdett called out, waving from the dining hall.

The cell-house count was carried out by six officers; each counted one of the tiers of B Block and C Block. On a signal from Lieutenant Simpson, each inmate stood silently at the door of his cell as the officers circled the block, then reported their count to Lageson.

"Total correct, Joe," Lageson advised Simpson. "Eight in the hospital, 23 in the kitchen, 26 in D Block, 223 in the main cell house, for a total of 280." Counts were an integral part of life on Alcatraz. There were fourteen regular counts of inmates in the cell house each day and seven shop counts during working hours.

As Lageson finished the count, he stopped in front of Coy's cell. Coy was sitting on his bunk in the neatly ordered cubicle, inhaling deep drags on his cigarette.

"Say, Bernie, the floors are looking pretty shabby this morning and need attention. Will you have time to wax them this afternoon?"

"Sure thing, Boss, I'll get right on it when the work crews leave this afternoon. I'll have everything shipshape by the time you get back from lunch."

Lageson had observed that Coy had been moody lately, not his usual friendly self. In fact, several of the normally friendly cons had seemed moody lately. That added to Lageson's apprehension. Today, however, Coy seemed to be in good spirits and, as always, was very cooperative.

I guess he had a good night's sleep, Ernie Lageson thought as he headed back to the west end of the cell house.

7

Across the cell house, Joe Cretzer paced back and forth in his cell, chain smoking from the abundant supply of hand-rolled cigarettes he kept on the shelf above his bunk. He let his mind wander—he'd been concentrating so hard on the upcoming events—to his family, specifically his two brothers. Although he thought of his brothers from time to time, he had not seen or heard from either of them in years. The last he had heard of them they were both serving time in eastern penitentiaries.

He also thought of his wife, Edna, living across the bay in San Francisco. They had been together for over fifteen years and had been brothel operators and bank robbers together. There had always been plenty of easy money, then. Now, as he returned to his bunk in the cool morning air, he was flush with excitement as he anticipated the break and his return to the good life. It won't be long, Babe, and we'll be back together in Frisco, Cretzer thought.

At 7:30 Lieutenant Simpson blew a whistle. The cells in B and C Blocks were opened. The prisoners stepped out. Following a second whistle, the convicts closed ranks and marched slowly to the dining hall, forming two lines as they entered and approached the steam table at the far end of the room. At the steam table each man picked up a steel tray and moved down the line to receive his food. The right line filed down the right side of the steam table, while the left line moved down the other side of the steam table. From the serving line the inmates proceeded to the nearest empty seats. There were ten seats at each table. Pitchers of milk, coffee, tea, and water and silverware, metal cups, and napkins had already been placed on the tables by the orderlies. As each man arrived at the table, he remained standing until the table was full. Then all ten took their seats and could begin eating. Talking was permitted, but loud or boisterous conduct was prohibited. On the morning of May 2, 1946, the breakfast consisted of oatmeal, toast, and fruit.

Not all the convicts ate in groups of ten. One inmate, a backwoodsman named Luscotoff, had such foul eating habits that the other inmates had all complained about having to eat with him. As a result, he sat at a table by himself, where he consumed his food in such a slovenly fashion that even the guards tried not to watch him.

Within minutes, the prisoners had all passed through the line and were seated. The entire meal took only thirty minutes. During the meal, ten guards circulated throughout the dining hall. From above, the room was under the surveillance of Bert Burch in the gun gallery.

During the meal service, Marvin Hubbard stood at the center of the steam table, serving those in the right line. As Coy picked up his tray, he and Hubbard exchanged knowing smiles.

Hubbard muttered under his breath, "Morning, Bernie. Looks like a good day for a boat ride."

The comment was audible only to Coy. It brought an even broader grin to the older man's face. "You said it, Marv," Coy replied. "Don't give me too much of that stuff. I've got to stay trim today."

As he turned down the line, Coy nodded politely to each of the inmate servers but declined everything but an apple and the oatmeal he had gotten from Hubbard.

Once breakfast service for the general population was underway, Officer Marvin Orr wheeled the portable steam cart out of the kitchen and into D Block. Orr was assisting today because of the recent D Block riot. D Block officer Cecil Corwin was uneasy and nervous that morning. He was just back from a two-week leave, and it was his first day as D Block officer in several months. He was happy to find that Lageson was the cell-house officer. Corwin felt comfortable with the younger officer in charge because of the quiet, confident way he controlled the inmates. None of the inmates challenged Lageson's authority. Breakfast service went smoothly.

After breakfast Corwin released orderly Louie Fleish from his cell to sweep down the area. Although Corwin was uneasy working in D Block, he liked the fact that the inmates almost never left their cells and there was an armed guard in the gallery above. Today, because of the earlier riot, there would be no yard time for any D Block inmates. Fleish would be the only inmate to leave his cell. In fact, Fleish was one of the few D Block prisoners Corwin was comfortable with out of his cell.

D Block, or isolation, was designed for those unable to comply with the rules of Alcatraz. This segregated area contained forty-two cells, six of which were solitary, unlighted cells referred to by guards and convicts alike as "the hole." The regular isolation cells were larger than the general-population cells because the prisoners in D Block rarely left their quarters. Once a week, those the administration felt could be trusted were permitted a one-and-a-half-hour recreational period in the yard. Because of the violent nature of so many of these men, only a few were permitted out of their cells at the same time. Frequently, only one D Block inmate at a time was permitted in the yard. A number of D Block inmates were never given yard privileges. Other than this periodic visit to the yard and a weekly shower, D Block convicts never left their cells.

Following an escape attempt, the would-be escapees were routinely incarcerated in D Block. The length of the stay depended upon the administration's view of each convict as an escape risk. Many inmates spent years in D Block following an escape attempt. Some were considered so misanthropic or violent that they never left D Block. Robert Stroud— the Birdman of Alcatraz—spent his entire seventeen years on Alcatraz in either D Block or the hospital. Confinement in isolation usually resulted from repeated misconduct or a serious breach of prison rules. Commitment to isolation came after a hearing before a disciplinary board that included the associate warden, the captain, and one or more officers. The inmate was advised of the charges against him, and he was given an opportunity to defend himself and explain his conduct. Only occasionally was an inmate's defense successful. D Block prisoners did not leave their cells for meals. Food was brought from the kitchen on portable steam carts. The trays were prepared by the D Block orderly under the supervision of the officer in charge and served to each convict in his cell.

As long as they did not deface the reading material, D Block inmates were allowed the same reading privileges as the general population. Every prisoner on the island was provided a reading list of titles and authors of the more than 15,000 volumes in the prison library. Books were delivered to the cells by an orderly. For the last few years, that orderly had been Bernie Coy.

The solitary cells were the most severe form of confinement on the island. Prison regulations prevented an inmate from serving more than nineteen consecutive days in solitary. However, occasionally an inmate would be released on the twentieth day, only to be returned the very next day for another stay of up to nineteen days. The solitary cells had two doors; the outer doors were made of solid steel, the inner doors were barred. With the outer doors closed, no light entered the cells. Light was admitted for twenty minutes three times a day during meal-times, when the outer doors were opened. Other-wise, the occupants were in total darkness. Five of the six cells contained a wall-mounted bunk, a toilet, and a sink/drinking fountain, but nothing else. At night a mattress and two blankets were provided but were removed in the morning. Inmates in the solitary cells wore nothing but prison coveralls and slippers. They were given no soap, no toothbrush, no tooth-paste, nor any other personal hygiene supplies ex-cept toilet paper. The prisoners were also not al-lowed to shave or shower during their stays in soli-tary.

The sixth of the solitary cells was a stripped cell, completely devoid of appliances, with only a hole in the floor for human waste. Occupants of this cell were often naked because they had destroyed their clothing and bedding. Confinement in the stripped cell was usually of short duration but could last up to three or four days.

Three meals a day were served to those in the hole. Breakfast consisted of four slices of bread and a bowl of coffee. Lunch included the bread and coffee, plus a bowl of soup. Dinner consisted of bread, a lettuce salad, and coffee or tea. Every third

day there was a full meal at noon, the same meal
that was served to all the other prisoners.

With breakfast over, the rest of the morning
should go quietly, Corwin thought. Except for some
final touch-up repairs to the cells damaged in the
riot, there were no unusual activities planned. Corwin anticipated a routine day. The only notable
event of the morning was Sam Shockley's recurring
complaint that the guards were poisoning his food,
putting minerals in his oatmeal. Like everybody else,
Corwin ignored "Crazy Sam."

Back in their cells following breakfast, the inmates prepared for the day. The outside crews
changed into work clothes. This was also the last
chance for each inmate to tidy up his cell and prepare for a possible surprise inspection during the
workday. Cells were always subject to shakedown
while the inmates were gone. They were also inspected for neatness and cleanliness during the day.
A prisoner whose cell was consistently untidy was
warned. If the situation didn't improve he was pun-
ished, either by the loss of privileges or the loss of
his job.

As long as a prisoner maintained a good record,
he was permitted to work as an indoor orderly, on
one of the outside details, or in one of the several
prison industries. To the extent possible, every inmate was encouraged to select his own work assignment. Work was a privilege, not a right. A work

assignment was one of the first things forfeited in the event of misconduct. Work was welcomed by nearly all the inmates. Not only did it help pass the time, but many of the jobs came with perks. Outside men could move around the island and often interact with the women and children living on the island. Kitchen workers got extra food rations and had the opportunity to secretly whip up a batch of home brew. Those in the prison industries got paid. They could send their earnings to their families or save for their release.

Personal hygiene consisted of daily sponge baths in the cells, although no hot water was available there. Hot showers were available on a weekly basis unless the inmate's work was of such a nature that more frequent bathing was necessary. In such cases, depending on the nature of his work, an inmate might shower daily. Shaving was permitted every other day and was accomplished by means of a double-edged safety razor issued to each inmate. Blades for the razors were distributed to each prisoner and collected after thirty minutes. The blades were resharpened periodically and stored on a board by the cell block so that each inmate was sure to get his own blade each time. Linens and uniforms were changed weekly, although, if conditions required, this could occur more frequently.

The general population worked five days a week, with Saturday and Sunday off. During their free time, the inmates could choose from an extensive selection of books, magazines, and other reading material maintained in the prison library. Prisoners were not permitted newspapers, radios, or any publications deemed inappropriate by the prison administration. If the library did not have a particular volume, the inmate could buy it himself if he worked at a job for which he was paid. Many of the inmates subscribed to art publications, magazines, and technical and legal journals.

There was no prison commissary. Very little eating was permitted outside the dining hall. Apples and oranges were the only food the prisoners were permitted to carry to their cells. Unlimited smoking was permitted. Any prisoner so desiring was issued a pipe and a generous supply of pipe tobacco. If they preferred, inmates were given cigarette papers and rough-cut tobacco to roll their own cigarettes. The vast majority of the inmates were smokers, and smoking was permitted in the cells, at work during breaks, and in the recreation yard.

Prisoners were permitted one visitor per month and two letters per week. All visitors and correspondents had to be preapproved by the prison administration and were generally, but not always, limited to immediate family. On weekend days the prisoners were permitted recreation time in the yard, where they participated in sports, dominos, and cards. Traditional playing cards were not permitted because the plastic coating on playing cards could be scraped off and used to create explosives. The inmates were, however, permitted to make their own cards and dominos out of wood. Some of the workmanship on these homemade items was exquisite. The completed sets were carried in handmade sacks and were highly prized. Church services were available, and movies were shown twice a month on Sunday afternoons.

Many of the convicts were accomplished artists or musicians and spent hours pursuing their hobbies. At one point a prison instrumental ensemble was formed. Instruments could be practiced in assigned basement rooms on weekends. Quieter instruments, such as guitars and harmonicas, could be played in the cells for an hour or so in the evening.

It was Officer Bill Miller's responsibility to see to it that the outside door was open when prisoners were ready to leave the cell house. He signaled Burch in the gun gallery to pass down key 107. Prison regulations required that after opening and closing the door, the key was to be immediately returned to the gallery. It would then be necessary to call for the key again the next time the door was to be opened. Some officers, including Miller, kept the key when they knew they would be opening and closing the door repeatedly rather than returning it to the gun gallery after each use.

Before the prisoners filed out, the civilian shop foremen and guards in charge of the work details took their positions in the yard. As the prisoners filed out of the cell house, they broke ranks, reassembled by work detail, and lined up ready to go to work. Once in line, the prisoners were free to talk and smoke while Miller conducted the count and Officer Al Shield obtained the key to the yard-wall gate from

Levinson in the Road Tower. Shield then opened the yard-wall gate and turned on the metal detector just outside the wall. This was a relaxed time, with prisoners and guards generally at ease and discussing the news of the day or the results of the professional baseball games played the night before. Because the prisoners were allowed no newspapers, the major news of the day was posted on a large blackboard in the dining hall.

With the count complete, a whistle blast signaled the work crews to file out of the yard, through the metal detector, and down the hill to the work areas at the west end of the island. The first and largest group to leave were the laundry workers. Fifty-eight men worked in the laundry, which occupied the upper floor of the industries building. At the sally port beneath the Hill Tower, the various crews split off and moved quietly to their respective shops. As they did, Officer L. L. Kelly marched the freight handlers and dock workers down the hill to the dock. The garbage crew, cleanup crew, and gardeners also mustered at the dock for their daily assignments.

The cell house at mid-morning was characteristically quiet. The custodial force was dramatically reduced, with only Miller and Lageson on the cellhouse floor, Burdett in the kitchen, and O'Brien, his duties in the kitchen complete, now in charge of the hospital for the rest of the morning.

As was his custom, Ernie Lageson took a brief

tour of the cell house to see that things were in order before he released the various inmate orderlies to their cell-house assignments. At the west end, he saw Bill Miller passing key 107 back to Burch in the gun gallery after having secured the door to the yard. Walking east along Seedy Street, Lageson heard his name called. He paused for a moment to identify the voice.

"Morning, Mr. Lageson. How's everything going?" It was the voice of Joe Cretzer, who was leaning against the bars of his cell door.

"Oh, hi Joe," Lageson said. "I didn't recognize your voice. Sounds like you've got a cold."

"Yeah, I guess it's something I brought with me from D Block, all that wind and cold."

Before entering the Navy, Lageson had been the D Block officer. He had come to know Cretzer quite well. During part of that time, Cretzer had been Lageson's D Block orderly, giving the two men considerable opportunity to spend time together. Cretzer was very intelligent and intellectually curious. He read a great deal. He was particularly fond of history and enjoyed discussions with Lageson, who had taught history. The two men developed a genuine respect for one another. Lageson had even discussed his relationship with Cretzer with his wife Eunice.

"This Cretzer has a fine mind and could be a success in anything he tried," Ernie told Eunice. "Unfortunately, the only thing he has attempted so far is crime, and by his standards, he has been highly successful. But even though he has read and studied a lot since he's been in prison, he still sees crime as his primary occupation. I really wonder if he'll ever be ready for life on the outside."

Philosophically, the men agreed on a number of subjects, but there was one upon which there was no common ground. Lageson and Cretzer studiously avoided any discussions of religion. Lageson had attended a Lutheran liberal arts college in Minnesota, and although he was a practicing Christian, he was by no means a zealot. Cretzer looked upon all religious faiths with disdain, considering religious belief a sign of weakness. But Cretzer also respected Lageson as a man and admired his intellect, strong personality, and physical prowess. There was nothing weak about Lageson.

"Hey, Joe," Lageson said, "isn't it about time you lined up a work assignment? It's been three months since you got out of D Block. Have you talked to the associate warden yet about a job?"

"Well, I've been thinking of maybe going back to the mat shop and seeing if I can make anything out of that assignment," Cretzer laughed.

Lighting a cigarette, Lageson was amused by Cretzer's reference to his ill-fated escape attempt. Then the officer's smiling face turned serious. He looked squarely into the convict's eyes. "You know, Joe, it's probably time you gave some serious thought to doing 'smart time.' You've got to admit there's no way of busting out of this place. God knows, there's plenty of guys that can attest to that, including you. You're still a young man. Hell, you're my age! You've got plenty of time to turn things around. You're smarter than most of the guys in here. If you'd set your mind to it, by the time you get out of jail you could easily have a college degree. You ought to consider getting a job in the library, where you'd be close to the books. Seems to me that's something that would appeal to you. Granted, it's not going to be easy, but guys do get out of jail and they do get off Alcatraz."

"Oh, I don't know, Mr. Lageson. I'm not convinced all that study shit pays off. Look at Stroud, that son of a bitch has been in jail all his life, and all his studying hasn't done him any good."

"Oh, come on, Joe. You're not like Stroud. He's too arrogant to change, and he just couldn't stop killing people."

"Well, I hear what you're saying, Mr. Lageson, but let's face it. I am what I am, and that's what I've been for the last twenty years. Change don't come easy, but I'll give it some thought. That library duty is a pretty cushy job. Who knows, maybe I'll be making some changes before too long. Thanks for your time, Mr. Lageson."

"Okay, Joe, see you later."

As he continued his tour of the cell house, Lageson ran the exchange again and again in his mind. What is it about men like Cretzer that keeps them from living normal lives? Maybe I've given Cretzer something to think about. But the years on Alcatraz had begun to take their toll on Ernie Lageson's optimism. Only Cretzer knew whether he would start doing "smart time" or continue fighting the system.

Following his tour of the cell house, Lageson

attended to his regular duties. He let Bernie Coy out of his cell and escorted him to the library so Coy could put together his magazine-and-book-delivery route for the morning. Lageson then released inmates Johnson, Testerman, and McDowell, who picked up their cleaning equipment from Thomas Wareagle, the A Block orderly, in preparation for sweeping down the cell-house tiers, stairs, and corridors. As the orderlies went to work, Lageson stopped by Wareagle's post to be sure that the cell-house orderlies had all the equipment they needed.

Thomas Wareagle was one of the oldest inmates on the island. He wore the number seventy-nine on his prison coveralls. Whatever Wareagle's true background—the old Indian had a variety of stories regarding his past—one thing was certain. He was no longer the man or the criminal he once had been. Now in his late fifties, significantly overweight and aching with arthritis, he was simply doing his time, hoping to someday make it back to the Osage reservation, where he would have been in line for tribal leadership if he hadn't deserted the reservation for a life of crime.

Wareagle frequently passed on bits of information to Lageson. He did not consider himself a stool pigeon since he never received any personal gain. He liked Lageson, and in his mind, he was simply making the boss's job a little easier.

Lageson spent idle moments with Wareagle. Frequently their discussions centered on the Lageson family. Wareagle enjoyed hearing about Lageson's young son and was always a ready listener when Ernie bragged about Ernie Jr. Although he had never even seen the boy, Wareagle felt he knew him. At Christmas each inmate was permitted to send two Christmas cards to just about anyone he chose, even if the individual was not on his approved list of correspondents. Wareagle's two Christmas cards always went to Lageson and Ernie Jr.

"How's everything going, Wareagle? Has everybody got plenty of cleaning gear?" Lageson asked.

"You bet, Boss. If those guys don't get this place cleaned up, it ain't this old Indian's fault. I'm also gonna have A Block looking real nice before lunch."

"Yeah, Wareagle, you don't want to miss that afternoon snooze in the sun," Lageson teased. "It's a pretty nice day, and you may not even need a coat out there today." Wareagle was entitled to an afternoon recreation period if all his duties were completed during the morning.

"No, these old bones need a coat, Boss."

After leaving Wareagle in A Block with his brooms and brushes, Lageson continued supervising the orderlies and cleanup crews in the cell house. He also checked on a crew of inmate painters painting empty cells. The late morning was a relatively quiet time in the cell house. Twelve cleaners were assigned to work in the cell house, sweeping, dusting, and mopping the floors and cleaning the windows. In addition, the kitchen crew was passed through for an hour or so of relaxation in their cells before they began preparing the midday meal. It was the joint responsibility of Lageson and Miller to pass inmates through to the basement, where Officer Ed Stucker supervised the clothing room, barbershop, storerooms, and showers. Finally, Lageson's morning activities involved some cursory cell inspections. He made it a point to check as many cells as he could to be sure that everything appeared in order and that the cells were neat and tidy.

As Buddy Thompson marched down the hill with his fellow tailor-shop workers, his thoughts were not of the upcoming workday. He studied the faces of those around him and smiled inwardly, smug in the knowledge that by this time tomorrow he, Bernie Coy, Joe Cretzer, and the others would be the primary topic of conversation among the inmates. He wanted to boast about what was soon to happen, but didn't. Without question, this would be the biggest day of his life.

Thompson learned of the escape plan just four months after he came to Alcatraz. Marv Hubbard approached him in the yard with an invitation to "go home." Thompson jumped at the chance and volunteered to do whatever he could to help. It was not until much later that a few of the details of the plan were explained to him.

To be in the cell house when the escape began, Thompson had to feign illness convincingly enough to cause shop foreman Haynes Herbert to grant his request for a "lay-in" that afternoon. Herbert was pretty mild-mannered and more trusting of the convicts than most of the other shop foremen; Thompson was confident he would believe the claim of illness. Thompson was less sure of his chances with Captain Weinhold and the medical technician. After an hour on the job, he motioned to Herbert, who came over to the tacking machine he was operating.

"I'm not feeling so good this morning, Mr. Herbert. I think I'm coming down with something. I think I'll go up to the hospital after lunch and ask for a lay-in slip this afternoon. Would that be okay with you?"

Just as Thompson had anticipated, Herbert's response was affirmative. "No problem, Thompson. I've got two tacking-machine operators, and I really only need one this afternoon. Kelly is available to operate the machine after lunch, so I can get by without you. Why don't you plan on taking a lay-in."

"Thanks a lot, Mr. Herbert," Thompson said. Now he had it both ways. He could seek a medical lay-in, and if he ran into any trouble with either the technician or Captain Weinhold, he could fall back on the fact that Herbert didn't have enough work for him in the afternoon anyway. He felt a rush of excitement at hearing Herbert's response.

Everything was set. In just a few hours, they would be making Alcatraz history.

8

At 11:30 the seagulls on the roof of the power-house were startled into flight by the shrill blast of the whistle. This signal marked the end of the morning work period. It alerted the convicts that they had just ten minutes to finish what they were doing and change out of their work clothing before the lines formed and everyone was marched back to the cell house for the noon meal.

In the cell house, Bill Miller and Ernie Lageson were slightly ahead of schedule and already had the entire staff of orderlies locked in their cells. The basement crews had been sent up early and were also in their cells. With everything in order and the outside work crews not expected for another twenty minutes, Lageson slipped into the chair behind the cell-house officer's desk and lit a cigarette. There were still a few inmates to be brought in from the yard before the work crews arrived. He had been on his feet all morning. It felt good to sit down.

As he sat quietly smoking his cigarette, Lageson's thoughts drifted again to Joe Cretzer. He wondered idly to himself what would become of the young criminal. His momentary solitude was interrupted by the voice of Miller suggesting that it was time to bring in the men from the yard.

"Yeah, Bill, let's get them in here. The work crews will be arriving soon, and we'll have enough to do then. Go get the key from Burch and let them in, and I'll go open their cells."

The sound of the powerhouse whistle shocked Joe Carnes out of his reverie. He jumped up quickly and stood at the door to his cell. Using his mirror, he looked up and down Michigan Avenue to see if Bernie Coy was anywhere around. The corridor was empty.

Earlier that morning, Coy had stopped at Carnes's cell. "Listen, Kid, we're goin' home this afternoon. If you want to go, you can. I'll open your cell when it gets started. If you want to go, just step out. If you don't, don't."

Now the young man paced back and forth in his cell, not knowing for sure if what Coy had said was true. He hadn't seen Coy since that conversation. He wondered what was going on. The young Indian returned to his bunk to try to relax and calm his excitement.

As the work crews mustered beneath the Hill Tower, Elmus Besk stood on the catwalk observing the activity below. In the Road Tower, Irv Levinson leaned on the railing, his Springfield rifle draped casually over one arm. Under the watchful eyes of the heavily armed tower guards, the long line of convicts snaked its way silently up the hill, shuffling feet and labored breathing the only sounds. Though work crews were permitted to talk while in outside marching formation, they were strangely quiet this morning. Once in the cell house, the inmates dispersed. Again, in uncharacteristic silence, they moved quickly into their cells. Following a five-minute rest and cleanup period, the mealtime procedure was repeated for the midday meal.

At his work station on the steam table, Marv Hubbard exchanged knowing glances with both Coy and Carnes as they filed by. Even though they were not in his serving line, Hubbard was also able to make eye contact with Cretzer and Thompson, who nodded and smiled as they turned to pass down the other end of the steam table. Hamilton, who was in the same line as Cretzer and Thompson, did not look in Hubbard's direction.

While the last few inmates filed into the dining hall, Lageson picked up the request slips from the small table by the door. Today there were several library-book requisitions, three applications for interviews with Associate Warden Miller, and nine requests for hospital visits during sick call after lunch. He passed the sick-call notes and interview requests on to Captain Weinhold. The library requests he put in his pocket to deliver to the librarian. The associate warden was not yet in the cell house but would be in Times Square as the prisoners filed out of the dining room.

Associate Warden Miller had worked his way up through the custodial ranks of the federal prison system, although he lacked a college education. He was a stocky man in his fifties with a receding hairline, booming voice, and dominating personality that served him well in his role as day-to-day supervisor of the prison. He was firm but fair in his dealings with the prisoners, but because his duties included overseeing inmate discipline, he was not well liked. Among the inmate population, he was known as "Jughead." His reputation as a harsh disciplinarian was partly due to his volatility. Following a disciplinary hearing, many an offending inmate heard his sentence meted out by the thunderous voice of Miller ordering, "Throw him in the hole!"

Today's noon meal was an inmate favorite, hot dogs and beans. Not only did the prisoners enjoy the food, but the beans created an opportunity for much well-worn and overworked humor. Twenty-five minutes after filing into the dining hall, the prisoners were marched back to their cells, where they stood by for yet another count. The afternoon schedule was somewhat varied, as certain prisoners were released from their cells immediately after the noon meal for sick call, meetings with the associate warden, and trips to the clothing exchange.

As soon as the prisoners were settled in their cells, Lageson opened the cells of those requesting sick call and those who needed to conduct official business. When his door slid open, Buddy Thompson hustled along the gallery and down the stairs at the west end of the cell block to become first in the hospital line. He was easily able to convince the medical technician on duty that his malady was legitimate. Within a few minutes, Thompson came down the hospital stairs carrying a small vial of pills and a lay-in slip to present to Captain Weinhold at Times Square. When the seemingly healthy Thompson presented Weinhold his slip, the captain mumbled an inaudible negative comment but signed the authorization.

At 12:30, Lageson began his busiest hour of the day. Miller left for lunch just as the count was beginning and there were several administrative activities to accomplish. Inmates needed to be passed from their cells to the clothing room, hospital, meetings with the associate warden, and haircuts in the basement barbershop. After the count and sick call, the work crews were marched out of the cell house.

While all these activities were going on in the main cell house, Orr was helping Corwin serve the noon meal in isolation. Fleish sat in his cell waiting for his tray like the other inmates. "You know, Mr. Corwin, this is really the shits, not letting me out to help with meals," he complained as Corwin served him his meal. Fleish didn't bother to point out that he hadn't taken part in the riot; group punishment was expected in prison.

"Yeah, Louie, I agree," responded Corwin, "but everyone gets a little upset when you guys bust up your cells. At least you'll be getting out after the meal is served, so it's not all bad," Corwin said.

Fleish's resentment faded quickly once his tray of food arrived. "Hey, beans and franks!" he exclaimed. "At least we got some good chow."

Following Officer Orr's departure, Corwin walked to the second tier and released Fleish. Fleish followed Corwin down to the flats and went to the storeroom to gather his cleaning equipment.

About 1:30, Corwin heard a knock on the cellhouse door. Looking through the small window in the door, he saw the familiar face of Associate Warden Miller. Calling up to Burch in the gun gallery, he obtained the key to the door and admitted the associate warden into D Block. Miller was there to interview two prisoners at their request. Robert Walker had requested that Miller release him from D Block. The associate warden had come to deliver the happy news that Walker could return to the general population. The other request came from Cliff Owens, who was asking to be made one of the D Block orderlies. Owens had been placed in D Block at his own request and for his own safety. He was known to be a stool pigeon and was a marked man. Making him an orderly would cause nothing but trouble for Owens and for the administration. Miller explained to him that it was never going to happen. "You'll take nothing but shit from the other inmates, Owens, and it just ain't worth it. Besides, you're scheduled to be released in three years, and enough people in here are jealous of that."

When his interviews were over, Miller returned to the flats and told Corwin that he was ready to leave. Corwin signaled for the key and opened the door. The associate warden left. Shortly after Miller's departure, the plumbing foreman arrived in D Block to check the riot repair work.

Guard Bill Miller returned from lunch just prior to the departure of the work crews, assuming his position at the outside door as they passed through. Again Miller did not return the yard key—key 107—to Burch after he locked the door but instead dropped it into his shirt pocket because he knew he would have to open the door several more times within the next few minutes.

With the outside work crews gone, Miller completed the one o'clock count, accounting for those prisoners remaining in their cells. He then passed Ed Stucker and his crew—including the inmate barber, clothing-room workers, and several men scheduled for haircuts and showers—into the basement and locked the door behind them.

The kitchen workers had their afternoons free and could either spend time in the recreation yard or in their cells. After completing their work in the kitchen, they simply walked through the dining hall to the cell-house door and were passed through and searched. They next went to their cells to change out of their uniforms. There were always a number of prisoners in idle status who were also entitled to yard privileges at this time. As he checked with the various idlers regarding their yard plans for the afternoon, Miller was surprised that both Cretzer and Carnes turned down yard time.

"Maybe there was a home-brew party last night and they're both hung over," Lageson said, laughing, when Miller mentioned it to him.

While Miller took the count and passed inmates out to the yard, Lageson checked with the orderlies to determine if their work was done and asked when they wanted to take their yard time. Wareagle chose to spend his afternoon in A Block. Librarians Cook and Baker indicated they would take their yard time when Lageson returned from lunch.

As he walked west along Broadway, Lageson heard the clanging of the main gate opening and closing. He looked around, surprised, and saw Joe Moyle entering the cell house. Moyle was one of the warden's four passmen, prisoners who worked as the warden's personal cooks and stewards. The passmen cooked and served meals to the warden and his wife and performed housekeeping tasks in their home. Moyle said he felt sick and had left work early to visit the hospital.

"Back a little early, aren't you, Moyle?" queried Lageson. "But there's no ball game this afternoon, is there?" On days when the Seals played in the afternoon, Mrs. Johnston let the prisoners listen to the game on the radio, defying the prison rules. The ball games were one of the many perks enjoyed by the passmen. Mrs. Johnston also permitted them to read the sports pages in the daily newspapers.

Moyle was a dark-haired, handsome young man. He was doing twenty-five years for bank robbery. He had been convicted in 1939 and sent to Alcatraz in 1941. During his seven years on The Rock, he had gained the respect of the administration. Moyle had the premiere work assignment on Alcatraz and would do nothing to jeopardize either his job or his chances for parole.

"You got it right, Mr. Lageson, they're playing tonight. I'll read about it in the Chronicle in the morning. I think I'm coming down with something, and I'm going up to the hospital. Is Mr. Miller at the west end to pass me up to the hospital?"

"Yeah, he's at the desk."

At the west end of the cell house, Miller opened the dining-hall door, then the door to the hospital. Moyle disappeared up the stairs. In less than ten minutes, he was back at the door knocking to get back into the cell house. Miller passed him through.

"Would it be okay if I went to the library and got a book before I go to my cell?" Moyle asked as he returned to the cell house. The warden's passmen were granted considerable latitude because of their good-conduct records. Miller did not hesitate in granting Moyle's request, forgetting, apparently, that the library was locked and that he had the key.

"Okay, Joe, just come back up here when you're ready to go to your cell and I'll open it up for you." As Moyle headed down Seedy Street, Miller resumed his seat behind the desk and lit a cigarette.

At the library Moyle found the door locked, although the librarian, Ed Cook, was working inside.

"Hey, Cookie, how do I get in there to do a little browsing?" Moyle inquired.

"You gotta get Miller to open the door for you. He's the only guy with a key. I'm a big deal around here, but they haven't given me my own set of keys yet," Cook said, laughing.

"Oh, shit!" Moyle shrugged. "I wanted to get a book this afternoon, but there's no way Miller'll come down here and let me in. I'll just have to wait for Bernie to get it for me tomorrow. Thanks anyway, Cookie. See you later."

9

The cell house was growing quiet. Ernie Lageson was about to leave for lunch. Bill Miller would soon be the only officer on duty in the massive room. Burdett would be the lone guard in the kitchen. Corwin would be alone in D Block, with Burch in the gun gallery above enjoying his post-lunch magazine review and siesta. This was exactly the situation for which Coy had planned. As he paced back and forth in his cell, Coy thought through each step in the plan one final time.

His concentration was interrupted by the sound of his cell door being racked open. The harsh noise startled him. He immediately realized that within a matter of minutes all his planning would become action.

Ernie Lageson was leaving for lunch. Coy could feel his heart racing. He stepped out into the empty expanse of Michigan Boulevard and walked rapidly to Times Square for his regular 1:30 meeting with "the Boss" to receive his afternoon instructions. Lageson was waiting for him. Looking at the officer holding his black-metal lunch pail, Coy thought to himself, Don't hurry back from lunch today, my friend, or it may be "lights out." All Coy said was, "Hey, Boss, what's up for today?"

"Like I said, Bernie, the floors look pretty bad today. I think they should be waxed. Did you finish all your library work this morning so you can go to work on the floors right away?"

"No problem, Mr. Lageson. You're right about the floors. They look pretty crappy. I don't know how these cons can screw up my nice waxed floors so fast. I should be able to get them all buffed by the time you get back from lunch. If they're not good enough, I can put down some more wax later in the day. What did the wife send you for lunch today?"

Lageson laughed. "I don't know, Bernie. Probably caviar sandwiches and a thermos full of champagne again. Do you have everything you need, or should we stop by A Block and see Wareagle?"

"I don't need anything from that old son of a bitch," Coy said, his voice nearly a snarl.

"Hey, Bernie, ease up on the old Indian. He's just trying to do his time."

"Well, between me and you, Mr. Lageson, I don't like the way he's doing his time. But he's your buddy, not mine."

As Lageson and Coy walked together down Broadway, the officer pointed out areas on the floor that needed special attention. At the cutoff Coy walked over to Seedy Street. Coy told Lageson that he was going to check the other corridor, then gather up his waxing equipment and go to work. Lageson proceeded to the east end of Broadway, then walked over to A Block for a final check on Wareagle. He saw the big Indian straightening shelves in one of the storage cells, appearing sufficiently busy to convince the officer that he was doing his job.

Satisfied with the conduct of both his inmate charges and comfortable that Miller had things under control, Lageson signaled to Phillips on the main gate to open up and let him out for lunch. It had been a busy morning. Lageson looked forward to thirty minutes of quiet in the administrative offices eating his lunch, perhaps letting his mind wander to thoughts of academia and teaching.

While Lageson and Coy were discussing the afternoon cleaning schedule, inmate kitchen workers were returning to the cell house. After each opening and closing of the rear door, Miller again and again dropped key 107 into his shirt pocket rather than passing it up to the gun gallery.

In his C Block cell, Floyd Hamilton lay on his bunk with his feet propped up on the sink, smoking a cigarette. He was deep in thought, wrestling, as he had for several weeks, with the question of whether he should participate in Coy's breakout. Initially Hamilton had been excited about the idea and had expressed his willingness to go along. Over the months that followed, however, he began to have second thoughts. He remembered the 1943 escape attempt and how sure he and the others were that the plan would succeed. The plans had been perfect down to the last detail, but the attempt had failed miserably.

Hamilton was one of the first prisoners Coy enlisted to participate in the break. As part of the scheme, Hamilton had reported to the hospital and obtained a medical lay-in so he could be ready to go when things got underway. But did he really want to try this again? Had the plan contemplated swimming to freedom, the answer was a simple no. But Coy's plan sounded good. The people were right. At times Hamilton believed they couldn't fail. On the other hand, he was thirty-eight years old with a bullet-riddled left leg. That and the high risk of failure made him ambivalent about participating. He would be forced to decide pretty soon, though. Within an hour his cell door would rack open.

After passing through the cut off, Coy did not return to the west end of the cell house. He instead turned left and raced to the east end of C Block. Peering carefully around the corner, he saw Ernie Lageson pass through the main gate and out of the cell house. As the main gate clanged shut, Coy stood for a moment, anticipating success. He spun around and raced to the west end of the cell house. There he grabbed the cement-filled buffer he used to shine the heavy wax on the cell-house floors and began pushing it across Times Square. Passing the dining-hall door, he peered in, looking for Hubbard. He saw Hubbard standing near the kitchen. Coy waved to him, indicating it was time to go.

Knowing that Coy had already received his instructions from Lageson, Officer Miller paid little attention to Coy as he began buffing down the floor near Times Square. Miller still had a few kitchen workers to pass out to the yard and a couple of inmates to send down to the basement for haircuts. He ignored Coy as the inmate pushed his buffer out of sight down Broadway. Coy quickly positioned himself out of Miller's view but visible to Hubbard in the dining hall.

After a final glance at the main gate to be sure there was no unexpected activity, Coy signaled to Hubbard to enter the cell house for his shakedown. Coy then noiselessly ran east down Broadway to the cutoff, through the cell block, and west along Seedy Street, arriving at the west end of C Block in time to see Hubbard emerge from the dining hall. According to plan, Hubbard stepped well into the cell house after passing through the gate and was careful to stand so that Miller was between him and Coy, now concealed behind the west end of C Block. As Hubbard positioned himself for the search, Coy took a final glance into the gun gallery to be sure Burch was still in D Block.

"You planning to go into the yard this afternoon?" Miller asked Hubbard.

"Naw, I just plan to sack out this afternoon,"

Hubbard replied, not giving Miller any reason to call Burch for the yard-door key. Hubbard couldn't have known that Miller had the key in his shirt pocket. The would-be escapees assumed that Burch had key 107, the key to the yard.

As he assumed the shakedown position, feet apart and arms extended to the side, Hubbard looked over Miller's shoulder for Coy. He heard no activity above. He assumed Burch was in D Block, but he couldn't see Coy. He tensed as Miller approached. He had expected Coy to intervene before Miller began the search. Hubbard felt the butcher knife he had slipped into his belt nestling against the small of his back. If Miller found the knife, it would all be over before it began.

With his back to the hidden Coy, Miller began the pat-down search. He ran his hands over each arm and across the shoulders. As he placed his hands on Hubbard's ribs and began probing his upper body, Coy dashed silently from behind C Block, covered the distance in an instant, and pounced on the unsuspecting officer from behind. Coy wrapped his right arm around Miller's neck and jerked him backwards with such force that the stunned guard's feet left the floor. At the same moment Hubbard sent a heavy fist crashing into Miller's face, then delivered a second crushing blow to his abdomen. The combination of punches dazed the officer, but he did not lose consciousness. Disoriented and off balance, he struggled valiantly to free himself. Two more shattering blows by Hubbard to

Miller's jaw rendered him unconscious. Miller slumped, a dead weight in Coy's arms.

"Nice work, Marv," whispered Coy. "He's out cold. Let's drag him down to the screws' toilet."

The end cell of C Block, cell 404, was unassigned and was used as the officers' cell-house toilet. Hubbard grabbed Miller's legs. The two men carried Miller the few feet from Times Square to cell 404, where they dumped the officer on the floor.

"Strip off his uniform and tie him up, Marv, then give me a hand with the bar spreader. I'll let Hamilton, Carnes, and Cretzer out. Don't waste any time. We've got a lot to do."

Reaching into the unconscious man's pants pocket, Hubbard pulled out a large ring of keys and handed them to Coy.

As Joe Moyle started back to the west end, a friend of his called out to him. He stopped to chat. He stayed there a few minutes, then continued west toward Times Square to report back to Miller. He saw what he thought was Miller at the west end of Seedy Street being carried by Coy and Hubbard. On the one hand, he was curious and wanted to go check it out. On the other hand, it was obviously trouble, and he didn't want to get involved. He paused for a few minutes until he saw all three disappear into the end cell. Hubbard had seen Moyle standing in the middle of the aisle and motioned him to come to the end of the block.

"C'mon, Joe, get into that first cell. You're not going to get hurt, just don't make any noise."

"Okay, Marv, whatever you say. What the shit's going on here?"

Hubbard didn't respond.

When Moyle arrived at cell 404, he saw Miller, unconscious on the floor of the cell with his hands tied behind him and his clothes lying on the bunk. Coy was holding a set of keys. Hubbard had a large kitchen knife stuck in the waistband of his pants. Coy left and disappeared around the end of C Block toward Times Square.

Coy pored over the bundle of keys and selected the one to the control box, which he had seen used so many times in the past. He rushed to the control box at the west end of C Block, unlocked the door and, with the skill of an experienced guard, maneuvered the levers to open Cretzer's cell. Thompson and Hamilton celled in the east end of the block. Their cells were controlled by an identical panel located there. Coy moved to the control box at the west end of B Block and moved the combination of levers that opened Carnes's cell. Next he raced to the east end of the cell house and released Thompson. In his haste he neglected to open Hamilton's cell.

Finally Coy went to the library and used Miller's key to open the door. "Hey, Cookie, let's go! This is it!"

In a couple of minutes, Cretzer arrived in front of cell 404. Hubbard handed him a pair of draftsmen's dividers that had been fashioned into a stiletto, with tape around the end to form a handle.

"Watch these guys, Joe," Hubbard directed. "I'm gonna go give Coy some help. He's going upstairs."

Moyle was extremely uncomfortable being in a cell with a hostage guard and asked Cretzer if he could go to his cell.

"You stay where you are, Moyle, and keep quiet!" Cretzer snapped.

Even though Cook had changed his mind and no longer wanted to join the escape, he decided to at least take a look. He followed Coy to the west end and looked into cell 404.

"Keep an eye on these guys, Cookie," Coy directed as he disappeared around the corner of C Block. Cretzer was in the cell with Moyle and the now-conscious Miller.

"What's going on?" Cook inquired.

"This is it," Cretzer said, backing out of the cell to face Cook, brandishing the homemade knife.

"Jesus Christ, I don't want any part of this!" Cook said.

"Hell, you can't back out on us now!"

"Back out? Shit, I'm not backing out. I was never in!" Cook turned to the guard. "Mr. Miller, I don't have anything to do with this. I don't know anything about it and don't want to know. I don't want any part of it." Cook turned and with a wave to Cretzer headed back to the library.

Nodding to Cook, Miller turned to Cretzer. "Joe, I think you're foolish to try this."

"Shut up, asshole!" Cretzer replied.

Moyle, standing in the back of the cell near Miller, squatted down in the corner and announced to no one in particular, "Boy, I picked a hell of a day to come back to the cell house early."

Moving quickly down Seedy Street to the library, Cook did not turn around or look back. Arriving at the library, he let himself in through the unlocked door and confronted his fellow worker, "Dub" Baker, working near the back wall.

"Stay in the library, Dub. Don't stick your head out that door. All hell's going to break loose. Coy is busting into the gun gallery."

With this warning Cook ducked down, out of sight behind a bookcase to wait it out.

Coy was out of breath from running back and forth the length of the cell house. He fumbled with the keys, trying to find the key to the C Block utility corridor. Finally he found it and swung the door open to peer into the dark, musty passage. Reaching into the darkness, under one of the floor beams, Coy found the heavy bag containing the bar spreader, pliers, and sack of grease. As he pulled the bag free he realized that his hands wcrc shaking. "Calm down, Old Man," he whispered to himself. "We've got a long way to go yet. Calm down."

Stepping back from the open corridor, Coy set the bag carefully on the floor and began peeling off his clothes. Before he took off his pants, he took the handcrafted tape measure from his pocket and slipped it into the bag. He was careful to stand close to the west wall and out of view of anyone looking out of the dining hall into the cell house. When he was down to his shorts and stocking feet, he pulled the sack full of heavy industrial grease out of the bag and began smearing it on his chest, shoulders, and the sides of his head and ears. Finally he applied a glob to his abdomen and spread it generously across his body. By now Cretzer had arrived. Coy handed him the sack of grease.

"Here, Joe, get my back and the back of my neck and shoulders." Cretzer coated Coy's back, and the nearly naked Coy was ready for his climb to the top of the gun gallery. Coy used a towel to wipe the grease from his hands. As he finished he looked up to see Hubbard carrying Miller's uniform.

"You took care of Miller, did you, Marv?" asked Coy.

"Yeah, Bernie, he came to but he's tied up good." Hubbard had brought a length of heavy twine from the kitchen, which he had used to tie Miller's thumbs and wrists together behind his back. He had removed the officer's necktie to tie his feet.

"Good. Toss that uniform over there on the floor. I'll put it on when I get back. Now give me a boost up onto the gallery bars."

Coy slipped the drawstrings of the bag over his left wrist, allowing him to use both hands for climbing. With a lift from Hubbard, Coy grasped the gallery bars and scrambled swiftly to the top of the gallery.

Stationing himself on the outside of the upper gallery in front of one of the spaces where the bars curved, Coy opened the bag and carefully removed the assembled spreader. He gingerly placed it between the bars, careful to line up the notched portions of the bolt and sleeve with the bars. He hand-tightened the nut until the spreader was firmly set. Next he removed the pliers from the bag, clamped them firmly over the bolt, and began to turn the bolt to spread the bars. It went easier and faster than he had expected. The layer of grease he had applied to the bolt provided ample lubrication for the nut. He only hoped that the bars would move far enough.

As he worked, he realized that he was covered with perspiration, including his hands and wrists. Drops were running down his forehead and face and into his eyes. Wiping the sweat from his face with the back of his hand, Coy looked down and saw Hubbard hanging on the front of the gallery just a few feet below to assist him if he needed help.

"How's it going, Bernie?" Hubbard whispered encouragingly.

"It's going great, Marv. The spreader's working fine. I should be done in just a few seconds."

As the spreader approached its limits, the amount of force necessary to turn the nut increased substantially. The pliers began to slip, and Coy was having trouble hanging onto the pliers because of the moisture on his hands. He wished he had brought the towel with him. All he had to dry his hands on was the bag and his shorts and socks. As he worked, he listened for Burch's return to the cell house but heard nothing.

Just as he had planned, he was able to move the bars from their original distance of just over five inches apart to slightly more than seven inches apart. After measuring the distance, Coy slowly eased back on the spreader to see if there would be any rebound movement once the spreader was removed. To his delight the bars stayed in place, over seven inches apart. He quickly removed the spreader and slipped it back into the bag for later use as a weapon.

Coy checked the tape measure one more time, then slid his feet and legs between the bars. Holding on with his arms, he began to wriggle his body through the opening. The grease on his slender hips helped. Within a few seconds he was halfway through the bars. As his chest passed between the bars, he exhaled and his upper body squeezed painfully between the steel strips. Now my head and my goddamn ears, Coy thought. He steadied himself by placing one of his feet against a crossbar on the front of the gallery. He twisted his body so that he now faced the front of the gallery. Pulling his head through was tight but easier than he had expected. His chest was raw and bleeding slightly in several spots, but he was through! He dropped catlike onto the gallery floor and stood motionless for several seconds, listening for sounds of Burch below. There was only silence.

Down on the cell-house floor, the others quietly celebrated Coy's success. Cretzer told them to keep quiet and stay close to the wall so they couldn't be seen from inside the dining hall or kitchen. Burdett was still in the kitchen and would come to investigate if he observed them moving around. Cretzer also told Carnes to maintain a lookout down Broadway in case anyone entered the cell house through the main gate.

Coy's face and upper torso were wet with perspiration. He moved quickly to the ladder and stepped down to the lower tier of the gun gallery. There was still no sign of Burch. The door to D Block was closed. He ran silently along the full length of the lower tier, clutching the spreader bag. Coy crouched beneath the small window in the middle of the D Block door. He listened carefully but heard nothing from the other side. He stood up and peered through the window but couldn't see Burch. He saw a rack of billy clubs, gas billies, and gas masks next to the door. Coy grabbed one of the clubs. He would use it to overpower Burch. But Coy didn't know where the gallery officer was, whether near the door or down on the main-floor level. Coy waited by the side of the door nearest the wall. The door was hinged on the side nearest the bars and opened into D Block, so Coy was poised to burst into D Block the moment the door began to move.

At about 2:00 Cecil Corwin was seated at his desk at the west end of D Block, chatting casually with Fleish. The weather outside had turned warm. Sunshine streamed through the windows and lent a cheery atmosphere to the otherwise grim cell block.

Suddenly there was a sound at the door like someone on the cell-house side knocking. Thinking it was the associate warden or the plumber returning, Corwin called for the key and casually opened the door. What he saw startled him. He quickly shut the door and relocked it. He saw Joe Cretzer near the dining-hall door talking to an inmate he didn't recognize and Joe Carnes standing in front of cell

404, with Bill Miller nowhere in sight. None of those men should be out of their cells at this time of day. What's going on? Where's Miller? A nervous man under normal circumstances, Corwin was suddenly in a panic.

10

Still waiting for Burch in the gun gallery, Coy finally saw the door begin to move toward D Block. As it did, he leaped forward, slamming the door back into the startled guard's face and knocking him against the bars on the D Block side. At the same time, he smashed the billy club into Burch's body. Burch bounced off the bars but held onto his rifle, which he threw up to catch most of the force of the crashing billy club. The frenzied force of Coy's blows drove the rifle into the side of Burch's head. Dazed, he stumbled backward as Coy grabbed the rifle. For a moment the two men struggled for control of the gun.

Coy swung the club again. This time Burch could not fend off the blow. He ducked his head, but the club smashed into the back of his neck. Burch dropped one hand from the rifle and attempted to draw his pistol. Moving backward along the gallery, Burch tripped over his lunch pail and fell onto his back, Coy landing on top of him. The rifle fell to the floor and skidded three feet away, beyond the grasp of either man.

Despite his shock and confusion, Burch had the presence of mind to shout out to Corwin below, "Get on the phone, Corwin! Get on the phone!"

Guard Cecil Corwin stared up at the gallery in horror. He was frightened and confused, but he backed further into the open area in front of the cells for a better view of the gallery. The steel shield across the bottom of the gallery obscured whatever was going on behind it. He looked over at Fleish for guidance, but read nothing in the convict's grim face. Up in the gallery, the ferocity of the struggle was escalating. He heard Burch calling him for help. "Get on the phone! Corwin! Get on the phone!" But Corwin stood frozen, paralyzed with shock and fear. Again, he looked pleadingly at Fleish for help. He saw only an icy stare.

The D Block convicts immediately began to shout and bang their metal cups on the bars. Some believed it was an escape attempt. Others thought the guards were beating a prisoner. As he continued to battle with Burch over the guns, Coy called out to the shouting convicts to quiet down, fearing the noise would alert guards outside D Block.

Fleish, seeing that Corwin was doing nothing, ran up the stairs to the top tier for a better view of the gallery. As he did, he called to those in their cells to be quiet. "Quiet down. There's someone in the gallery fighting with Burch! It must be a break!" From the top tier, he still had no view of the floor of the gallery and so returned to the flats. He found Corwin in the middle of the cell block, rigid with fear, staring blankly at the gallery.

"There's somebody up in the gallery fighting with Burch," Fleish repeated, but Corwin didn't seem to hear the comment. The color was gone from the officer's face. His hands were trembling.

Burch struggled to escape. He managed to roll onto his left side, trying to keep his body between Coy's grasping hands and the pistol. He was able to pull the pistol from the holster, but Coy ripped it from his hand. Again, neither man could control the weapon and it bounced harmlessly away. As they scuffled, Coy was still on top of Burch. Coy grabbed the older man's arm and twisted it behind his back into an excruciatingly painful hammerlock. Burch was suddenly totally helpless. Coy beat Burch mercilessly on the back of the head, still applying bone-breaking pressure to his twisted arm. He then began choking Burch with the guard's own tie and shirt collar.

After a few minutes, he felt Burch's body go limp. Coy quickly dragged Burch's unconscious body through the door and into the main cell-house side of the gallery. He stripped off Burch's gun belt and ammunition pouches and scooped up the guns from the D Block side. Below he could hear Cretzer calling excitedly, "Sounded like a hell of a fight up there, Bernie. Did you kill him?"

"I don't know, but he's out cold. He won't bother

us anymore. I'm going to tie him up. Here, take this other stuff."

Cretzer stood on the cell-house officer's desk and reached up so Coy could pass down the two guns, pouches of ammunition, clubs, gas billies, and gas masks. "I hope we don't need these things," Cretzer remarked as he accepted the gas masks.

"This is fucking great!" Joe Carnes said, taking one of the highly polished billy clubs. "I might just get me a screw with this."

Hubbard held the rifle, checking to be sure it was loaded. Cretzer fondled the .45-caliber automatic pistol as if it were a work of art.

After passing the weapons down, Coy pulled off Burch's shoes and removed his trousers and uniform coat. Next he gathered up all the keys and dumped them on top of the coat with the trousers, wrapping them all up tightly. He wedged the bundle through the bars, dropping it to the floor below. He then returned to the unconscious guard. With the cord used to pass keys down to the cell-house floor he tied Burch's hands tightly behind his back. He then passed the cord around an electrical conduit pipe on the gallery wall and tied Burch's head and neck to the pipe. As Coy tightened the line around the guard's neck, Burch flinched instinctively. He's still alive, Coy thought. I'd better tie him up good so if he comes to, he can't turn in the alarm. He wrapped the cord twice more around the pipe and Burch's neck, then tied the knot behind Burch's head. Finally, he removed Burch's necktie and used it to bind the guard's feet together.

With the struggle over, D Block fell silent. Even the convicts were quiet, busily focusing their mirrors to get a view of the gallery.

Within moments there was a banging on the cell-house door and the muffled voice of Joe Cretzer. "Corwin," he yelled, "get this goddam door open, and be quick about it!"

Corwin moved cautiously toward the door and slid open the steel panel covering the window. He saw Cretzer holding a pistol and Hubbard standing behind him with a rifle. Fleish looked over Corwin's shoulder, saw what was going on, and retreated, fearing that the gunmen would start shooting.

Again Cretzer demanded: "Get this goddam door open, Corwin, or I'll blow your fucking head off!"

"What should I do, Louie?" Corwin asked. His voice was cracking. His lower lip was quivering. His eyes were full of fear.

"You better open the door, Mr. Corwin, there's nothing else you can do. They got guns out there. Those guys'll kill you if you don't."

Corwin's hands were shaking as he fumbled with the key and tried to insert it into the lock. At the same time, Fleish retreated even further away from the door. As the door swung open, Cretzer grabbed Corwin and threw him across Seedy Street toward cell 404. Then Cretzer and Hubbard rushed into D Block, waving their guns and swaggering to the area in front of the cells.

Looking up at the second and third tiers, Cretzer shouted: "We've taken over this fucking joint!

Where's Franklin? Hey, Whitey, where the hell are you?"

From the bank of cells in front of Cretzer, a voice called out, "Franklin's in the hole. He's in cell number 9."

"Hey, kid," Cretzer called to Carnes, who was standing guard in front of the hostage cell. "Bring Corwin back in here." Carnes did what he was told and delivered the frightened guard to Cretzer at the west end of the block.

"Come here, Corwin," Cretzer ordered. He grabbed Corwin by the arm and pressed the muzzle of the pistol to his temple. Cretzer pushed him down the cell block to the solitary cells, stopping in front of cell 9. "Open this cell and let Franklin out!" he demanded.

"I can't," Corwin responded weakly. "My key only opens the outer door. The inner door is controlled from the gallery."

"Oh, shit! That's right!" Cretzer said. "I remember that from when I was in the hole."

Corwin opened the outer door. The afternoon sun streamed into Franklin's dark cell. Franklin came to the door and squinted out, temporarily blinded by the light.

"Sorry, Whitey, we ain't got time to go back up in the gallery and let you out of there. Too bad you can't come with us. I guess you shouldn't have busted up your cell last week. I'll leave the door open for you so you can get some light in there. Hey, I'm really sorry, buddy."

"Well, shit, Joe!" Franklin said. Then his shoulders

sagged. "That's okay, Joe, I understand. Good luck, guys. Wish I was going with you, but I understand."

Cretzer turned and headed back to the cell-house door, pushing Corwin ahead of him. At the west end of the block, Cretzer said to Fleish, "Hey Louie, get some smokes to Whitey, will you?" Without waiting for an answer, Cretzer shoved Corwin toward the stairs at the end of the tier, demanding that he open all the cells on the two upper tiers. The frightened officer haltingly climbed the steps to the second tier, then to the third. At both levels he operated the levers in the control boxes to open all the cells. As the cell doors banged open, the inmates cautiously stepped out of their cells, milling about on the tiers. A few descended the stairs to the flats. Some returned to their cells.

In the gun gallery, Burch returned to painful consciousness. As his head cleared, he became aware of the throbbing pain at the base of his skull, where he had taken the full force of Coy's billyclub blows. His head and hands were tied to an electrical conduit mounted on the wall, but he was able to free himself with relative ease. He lay on the floor for a few moments, then crawled back to the D Block side of the gallery.

Carnes left his post in front of cell 404 and wandered into D Block with the homemade shiv in one hand and a billy club in the other. "So this is D Block," he mused, looking around. "I've heard a lot about this place. It don't look much different than the cell house to me."

"Say, Joe, you don't think this guy turned in the alarm before we got the door open, do you?" Hubbard asked Cretzer.

Again placing the barrel of the pistol against Corwin's head, Cretzer repeated Hubbard's question. "Did you turn in an alarm, Old Man?"

"No! No! I didn't," Corwin insisted.

"Are you sure, you son of a bitch?" Cretzer pressed the gun tighter against the terrified man's head.

"Honest, no!" pleaded Corwin. "Ask Fleish. He was here the whole time. He can tell you I didn't turn in any alarm."

"Is that right, Louie?" Cretzer asked Fleish as he released his grip on Corwin and removed the gun from his head.

"Yeah, he didn't go near the phone," Fleish assured him. "I couldn't believe it, but he didn't even try to call."

"Okay, Kid, get him out of here and put him in the toilet with the others," Cretzer told Carnes. He contemptuously pushed Corwin toward Carnes, who led the guard by the arm to cell 404. As Corwin stumbled into the cell, he moved to the right rear corner and leaned against the wall.

Cretzer ran up the stairs to the top tier of D Block and stood in front of Henri Young's cell. The door was open. Young was sitting on his bunk. Believing he was about to die at the hands of an avowed enemy, Young stood up and walked directly toward

Cretzer, who pointed the pistol at Young's head. There had been bad blood between the two former friends ever since Young was baptized a Catholic. One afternoon in the yard, a philosophical argument between the two became violent. Young, the devout Christian, was the undisputed victor. Cretzer was enraged. The outcome of the clash had haunted Cretzer for years since he clung to the view that all religious men were weak. Now he had the opportunity to blow Young away. "I ought to kill you, you fucking Catholic pussy, but I don't want to waste a bullet on you." With that Cretzer smiled and walked away. Young retreated slowly and settled back on his bunk.

Cretzer had taken only a few steps back toward the stairs when he saw Burch peer over the steel shield of the gallery. Cretzer snapped off a shot, missing his target. Burch disappeared below the shield.

"Stay down, you son of a bitch, and stay away from that phone or I'll blow your goddam head off!" Cretzer yelled, then stormed down the tier and descended the stairs to the flats.

After Cretzer returned to the main cell house, the D Block inmates began to chatter nervously among themselves. A large group collected at the cell-house door but remained in D Block. A few announced that they intended to join the escape. Others expressed shock over how the escapees had obtained guns and speculated as to what they were going to do next. For all their talking, none of the D Block inmates attempted to join the escapees except "Crazy

Sam" Shockley, who ran crazily around D Block and the main cell house, trying to become a part of whatever was going on. As usual, he was ignored by everyone.

When Coy burst into the gun gallery, Shockley was one of the first inmates to start shouting. He was also the only inmate to continue to yell and bang his cup on the bars after Coy ordered everyone to quiet down. As the cell doors opened, he was one of the first to dash out. He ran immediately into the main cell house, where he stared stupidly at the hostages in cell 404 before running back into D Block. His shoes had been confiscated, and he was barefoot. Enjoying his first taste of freedom in eight years, the crazed convict ran back into the main cell house. He stared with wild eyes at Cretzer and Hubbard and the guns in their hands. "Can I go too, Joe?"

"Sure, Sam," Cretzer said. "Just stay out of the way and keep quiet. I'll tell you when we go."

Shockley went into a frenzy. He spotted a heavy pipe wrench, abandoned by Cretzer in favor of the pistol. Shockley grabbed it and charged back into D Block. He entered the first cell he came to, the D Block officers' toilet, and began smashing the plumbing fixtures. Within seconds he had completely smashed the porcelain toilet and sink. "Look, I'm still busting up stuff!" he shouted with demented glee. "We're breaking out of this place! We're breaking out!" Shockley became maniacal, completely out of control. After smashing everything he could in the toilet cell, he ran back into the cell house, sweating and laughing all the while. "Look, I'm still breaking up stuff!" he repeatedly babbled to anyone who would listen.

11

In the administration offices, Chief Steward Robert Bristow had just finished the menus for the next three days. Bristow had no custodial duties but supervised all the culinary activities in the prison. With the weekly paperwork out of the way, Bristow headed back to his small kitchen office. He passed through the main gate and walked absentmindedly down Broadway. At the west end of the cell house, he was suddenly confronted with a confusing situation. On the floor just to the left of the dining-hall door he saw an officer's uniform and a set of keys. To his right, behind the end of B Block, stood Clarence Carnes with an object in his right hand that Bristow could not identify. And he saw Marvin Hubbard hanging on the bars of the west gun gallery, eight feet above the floor. Bill Miller was not at his normal post.

Of course, Bristow realized that something was terribly wrong. He looked for Bert Burch in the gun gallery and instead saw Coy on the lower tier. Before he knew what was happening, Carnes grabbed Bristow, placed a sharp object to his throat, and instructed him to move over to the wall under the gallery. As Carnes pushed him across Times Square, Bristow saw Coy handing guns down from the gallery. He couldn't believe what he was seeing.

"Put him in cell 404 with the others," Coy ordered from the gallery.

Without speaking, with the sharp point pressed firmly against Bristow's throat, Carnes guided the befuddled steward around the west end of C Block and into the cell with Moyle and Miller. Once in cell 404 Bristow stared with astonishment at Miller, who was bound at the hands, wearing no pants or jacket.

"How did this happen, Bill?" Bristow asked.

"I don't know, Bob," Miller answered. "They jumped me, took my uniform and keys, and tied me up in here. I don't even know how many of them are involved. It's not good." Bristow looked questioningly at inmate Moyle, but neither man spoke.

Inmate painter Earl "Lefty" Egan stepped out of the C Block cell he was painting for a cigarette break. As he walked west down Broadway, he sensed something unusual. The cell house was much too quiet. Reaching the west end, he saw Hubbard holding a rifle and Cretzer standing next to him waving an automatic pistol. "Holy shit!" Egan whispered. "What the fuck is going on?"

Looking up at the gun gallery, he saw the nearly

naked Coy tossing an ammunition belt of rifle shells down to Hubbard.

As he dropped the belt, Coy saw Egan staring up in disbelief and called to him. "Hello, Lefty, you want a part of this?"

"Hell no, Coy, this is way too tough for me." Egan stood still, waiting for instructions. Then he made eye contact with Cretzer.

Cretzer motioned Egan with the pistol. "Come over here, Lefty."

Egan followed Cretzer to cell 404, where he joined the others. Seeing the other occupants of the cell, Egan called out, "Hey, Joe, how about putting Moyle and me in another cell?"

Cretzer ignored the request and turned away. The four captives stood motionless, staring silently at one another.

The stillness was suddenly shattered by the sound of the cell door opening. Carnes pushed Corwin into the cell. The door banged shut but did not lock. Concerned for his own safety yet feeling far better off than the officers with whom he was confined, Egan warned, "Don't do anything stupid to piss these guys off or you'll get shot." From the looks on their faces, Egan was satisfied that none of the prison employees were feeling like heroes.

By now Coy had returned to the cell-house floor. He quickly put on Burch's trousers, then checked cell 404, taking inventory of the hostages. Cretzer smiled at seeing his friend wearing a guard's "monkey suit." Gathering up all the keys, Coy spread them out on the cell-house desk. He directed Cretzer and Thompson to locate key 107 and unlock the door to the yard. He stationed Carnes and Hubbard as lookouts down Broadway. "Everything is going great," Coy said. "All we've got to do is find that key and we're ready to go."

"It ain't here, Bernie," Thompson lamented. "Maybe that's the wrong number. Are you sure it's 107?"

"Damn right," Coy said. "Try them all till you find the one that opens the door. We should have all the keys in the cell house."

Ernie Lageson sat at the conference table in the reception area of the administration offices, finishing his last cup of coffee and reading the morning Examiner. He glanced at his watch as he returned the thermos to his black-metal lunch pail and looked toward Carl Sundstrom's desk.

"Well, Sunny, it's after two, so I guess I'd better head back to the jail. Bill Miller's gonna be looking for me if I don't get back there pretty soon." Sundstrom, the prison record clerk, was typing a writ for one of the inmates.

Lageson was in no particular hurry to return to the cell house. After all, things were rather quiet at this time of day, so he loitered a few minutes chatting with Phillips and Fish. It was after 2:10 by the time he headed back to his post.

Entering the cell house, Lageson was surprised to find Wareagle at the west end of A Block rather than working at the east end, as he usually did this time of day. "Everything okay, Wareagle? Any problems?"

"No sir, Boss, everything's fine. Just doing my job down here and being a good Indian."

Wareagle was troubled. Even he had heard rumors of a coming "blastout." His position in the social strata of the prison did not favor him with sensitive information. There were always rumors of escape attempts, most of which an experienced convict like Wareagle ignored. Recently, however, he had overheard some comments about Coy that caused him to believe that something big was in the works. So today, when he heard unusual activity in the vicinity of Times Square, then heard Carnes's cell door unexpectedly open, Wareagle climbed to the upper tier of A Block for a better view of the action. He saw Coy in the gun gallery, Hubbard hanging on the outside, and lots of activity at the west end. Then he saw both Cretzer and Hubbard with guns. The rumor was true. A blastout was underway. Convicts at the west end of the cell house were armed with guns from the gallery.

In any prison the days are as gray as the prisoners' uniforms. An escape is an exciting event. Generally that would have been Wareagle's attitude, too, but not this time. He dreaded having to see Lageson. He had hoped to avoid having to even speak to Lageson when the guard returned from lunch. That's why he had busied himself at the far end of A Block. But now he faced his friend under ugly circumstances.

He liked Lageson. The young officer had always

treated him like a man rather than the loser he thought he was. As Wareagle stood making small talk with Lageson, he had difficulty making eye contact, knowing the danger Lageson was facing. The old man was ill at ease and shifted his weight from one foot to the other, avoiding Lageson's eyes. Although Wareagle had been able to pass some information to his friend without calling too much attention to what he was doing, he could not let Lageson know about the blastout underway. If he warned Lageson and Lageson sounded the alarm, Wareagle would be a walking dead man.

The life of a prison guard taken hostage during a break was worth little. Soon Lageson would be a hostage. It made Wareagle ashamed of his silence. Finally, unable to face the unsuspecting Lageson any longer, he turned away. "I better get back to work, Boss. I gotta lot to do back here."

"Okay, Wareagle, see you later," Lageson responded genially, oblivious to what was waiting for him. He locked the gate and walked down Broadway toward the west end of the cell house.

It was almost 2:15. The orderlies would be anxiously awaiting his return. As Lageson crossed Broadway en route to the control box at the east end of C Block, he noticed that the floor had not been waxed. He wondered why. Where is Coy? At the cutoff, he saw the buffer against the wall and said it out loud, "Where in the hell is Coy?"

Glancing west down Broadway, Lageson saw a group of men standing at Times Square. One of them looked like Coy, but without a shirt on. Think-

ing there might be a fight in progress, he broke into
a run. It had to be trouble of some kind. As he
neared the west end of the cell house, he saw Coy
coming down Broadway to meet him. Naked from
the waist up, Coy was wearing officer's trousers and
had traces of grease and blood on his chest and
shoulders. As they met, he grabbed Lageson by the
left arm and began leading him to the west end of C
Block. Lageson pulled his arm free and as he did
Coy said, "Mr. Lageson, this is it. Don't be a goddam
fool."

As he pulled away, Lageson suddenly realized
what was going on. From his right, behind B Block,
Hubbard stepped out pointing the rifle at him. From
his left Joe Cretzer came with a guard's pistol in his
hand. Behind Cretzer was Carnes with a billy club.
Looking past Cretzer and Carnes, he saw Fleish
standing in the D Block doorway. Coy is right,
thought Lageson. This is definitely it.

Lageson's immediate reaction was confusion and
disbelief. Where's Miller? They must have gotten into
the gallery and taken Burch's guns. Where's Burch?
Seeing the door to D Block open confused him.
Where's Cec Corwin? Are they all dead?

As he began to accept the reality of the situation,
Ernie Lageson had the sinking realization that he was
probably going to die. Although he got along well
with Coy and Cretzer, under these circumstances he
had no idea what to expect from either man. With a
gun in hand, neither was the same man Lageson
knew. He didn't know if he could talk logically with
them or if they had drifted into some realm of

Alcatraz Island Prison as it appeared in 1946 with San Francisco in background. *San Francisco Maritime NHP (National History Park)*

The Lagesons—Ernie Sr., Eunice, and Ernie Jr. in 1946. They lived in civilian housing on the island from 1941 to 1943.

Ernie Sr. in Alcatraz Prison guard uniform, 1946.

Building 64 on Alcatraz Island which housed civilian families. Windows of the Lageson apartment are shown on the second floor, far right, rear of the building. The homes of the prison warden and physician are shown at the top of the photo.

Bernard Coy

Joseph Cretzer

Sam Shockley

Marvin Hubbard

Clarence Carnes

"Buddy" Thompson

The west gun gallery where Bernard Coy scaled the bars and broke in. He squeezed through the bars at the top level after parting them with a homemade bar spreader.
San Francisco Maritime NHR

Coy's bar spreader which he had made in the prison machine shop. He placed the notched ends against the bars, then forced them apart by turning the nut with a pair of long-handled pliers. Coy was able to move each bar about an inch, creating an opening large enough for him to slip through. *San Francisco Maritime NHP*

A patrol boat with Marines standing in the bow sits to the east of Alcatraz Island, ensuring that none of the convicts escaped to the mainland. *San Francisco Chronicle*

Smoke and flames billow from windows of the main cell block at Alcatraz as prison personnel and U.S. Marines launch an assault on the six inmates inside who refuse to surrender. A guard (circled) on the ramp outside the cell block hurls tear gas bombs through the shattered window. *UPI/Corbis—Bettmann*

Warden James A. Johnston at the door that stopped the escape. The door, leading to the recreation yard, could have been opened with Key 107. However, by chance, Guard Bill Miller kept the key in his pocket that day, rather than returning it to the key case. *UPI/Corbis*

Warden James A. Johnston in front of cell 403 where inmate Joseph Cretzer shot hostages Lageson, Corwin, Miller and Weinhold. *UPI/Corbis—Bettman*

The utility corridor in C block where inmates Coy, Cretzer and Hubbard died. Their bodies were found here after the uprising. *San Francisco Maritime NHP*

Associate Warden Edward J. Miller, shown with facial burn he received when a tear gas canister exploded in his face as he ran from the cell house, after being shot at by inmate Marvin Hubbard. *UPI/Corbis—Bettman*

Inmates Thompson, Shockley, and Carnes, handcuffed and chained together, en route to court for arraignment on murder charges following their escape attempt. *San Francisco Maritime NHP*

frenzy. Convicts with guns loose on the island! Once out of the cell house and over the yard wall, there was nothing to keep them from going into the dependent's quarters below, where the women and children were. For a fleeting moment he thought of his wife and son and the fact that they were not at risk. Alcatraz convicts had killed before in order to escape. They were capable of killing again. Ernie sighed. With the convicts armed, it was certain that somebody would die.

Cretzer motioned with the pistol for Lageson to accompany him toward D Block. Just then Joe Burdett emerged from the dining hall and was taken with Lageson to cell 404. As they reached the cell, Shockley ran at Lageson, waving his arms as if to attack him. Screaming obscenities, he lunged at the officer, swinging wildly with closed fists. "I want that fucker's ass. He slugged me the last time I threw my stuff out. I want his ass, Joe." Cretzer stepped between Shockley and Lageson and leveled the pistol at the charging inmate.

"Back off, Sam. We don't have time for this kind of shit. If Mr. Lageson hit you, you probably had it coming. Now back off!"

"I want him, Joe. I want his ass," whined Shockley, cowering before Cretzer's will, and the pistol.

"Goddammit, Sam, back off or I'll put a hole between your fucking eyes!" Cretzer hissed, pointing the pistol at Shockley's head. "We've got a long way to go, and we need these guys alive." Shockley backed away, staring angrily at Lageson.

As Lageson turned to enter cell 404, Cretzer

handed him a bundle of keys. "Go up and get Hamilton out of his cell," Cretzer directed. "Hey, Floyd! We're coming to get you!" Hamilton's answer was inaudible.

But Lageson didn't take the keys. He said in a firm, unemotional voice, "No, Joe, you go get him yourself."

Coy, standing behind Cretzer, heard the exchange and tried to intervene. "Don't be a fool, Mr. Lageson. Do as he says."

Lageson ignored Coy and directed his gaze at Cretzer. "You can lock me up or do whatever, I'm not going to go get Hamilton. Get him yourself."

It was a tense moment as Coy, Carnes, Thompson, and Hubbard all watched Cretzer. He hesitated, gun in hand. It was a one-on-one matchup for Cretzer. He was suddenly faced with the reverse of the situation he had experienced so many times with Lageson. On prior occasions in their discussions they had frequently taken contrary positions. On every such occasion, Cretzer had been treated by Lageson with courtesy and respect. Now Cretzer had made a demeaning demand of the officer. Lageson had refused to be intimidated. Cretzer's initial reaction was negative. He was in the driver's seat. He was in control. Yet he hesitated. He found himself unable to treat Lageson any differently than the officer had treated him on so many occasions in the past.

"Okay, Mr. Lageson, have it your way. I'll go get him myself." Cretzer left to release Hamilton himself.

The exchange infuriated Carnes, who by now

had become quite aggressive and was cursing at the guards at every opportunity. "You fucking screw," he snarled. "We're in charge here now!"

Again Coy intervened. "Calm down, Old Man. It's not important. Let's keep our minds on what we're doing here." With that he pushed Lageson into cell 404, which by now was getting crowded.

Miller's hands were still tied. Bristow asked if he could untie him.

"Sure, go ahead," snapped Carnes, eager to exercise his authority. "He ain't going anywhere now." Bristow untied Miller, who rubbed his hands and wrists to stimulate circulation.

After Lageson entered the cell, Coy slid the door shut and tried to lock it. But the door couldn't be locked. "Goddammit, let's get these guys into a cell that we can lock," Coy said.

As Coy fiddled with the cell door, Moyle and Egan moved to the front of the cell and again requested that Coy put them in a cell by themselves. Both of them knew what would probably happen to the hostages and wanted to be as far away as possible.

With his hands now free, Miller moved unobtrusively to the back of the cell. He reached into his shirt pocket and pulled out key 107—the key to the recreation yard, the key Coy and the others were so desperately searching for. He handed the key to Burdett and whispered, "Here, hide this someplace. They got all my other keys, but they didn't get this one. Without this, these assholes can't go anywhere." But there wasn't any place to hide the key except under the bunk. Burdett slipped the key as far under the bunk as he could without being observed by any of the convicts.

Egan called out again since they still had no response from Coy, who was preoccupied with trying to lock the cell door. This time he called out to Cretzer, now back in front of the cell. "Come on, guys, let me and Moyle change cells. We don't want to be in here with all these screws."

"Yeah, okay," Cretzer responded. "Go down to my cell, 397. You can hang out there."

Coy was still muttering about the door. He finally ordered all the officers out of cell 404 and into cell 403. The door was again opened. The five officers slowly moved into the next cubicle. In the new cell, Lageson and Corwin ended up in the rear. Lageson sat on the toilet. Corwin leaned against the back wall. Miller and Bristow sat on the bunk mounted on the west wall. Burdett leaned against the east wall opposite the bunk. Nobody spoke. Each man was absorbed in his own thoughts.

Lageson accepted the fact that he was about to die. "Please, God," he prayed. "However it goes, let it be quick."

"This is it, isn't it, Ernie?" Corwin asked in a quavering voice.

Lageson turned and looked into the dispirited face of Corwin and saw the fear in the older man's eyes. "It doesn't look good, Cec."

Corwin was a gentle man, almost old enough to be Lageson's father. The two men stared hopelessly at one another for several moments in silence.

"Where's Burch?" Lageson finally asked. "They've got his guns."

"I don't know," Corwin said. "I think he's dead. There was a hell of a fight in the gun gallery. Then I didn't hear anything. I think Coy killed him."

"How in the hell did they get into the gallery?" Lageson asked.

"I don't know, Ernie. All of a sudden they came storming into D Block, guns and keys. I couldn't believe it."

Just then Joe Cretzer stormed up to the door. "Miller," he yelled, "which fucking key opens the yard door?" Miller looked around at the other guards to see what he should do, but nobody would raise his eyes.

"Number 107," he said finally.

"Shit, that's what we thought, 107! Where the fuck is it? We've got no key 107."

"I don't know," Miller said. "You've got all the keys."

Cretzer hurried back to the cell-house desk and the collection of keys. Thompson was frantically trying different keys in the lock, but nothing worked. There was no key 107.

"We ain't got no 107," Thompson said. The voices were now interrupting one another and getting louder and more frustrated. The officers could hear the clanking of keys but couldn't make out what was being said. A few minutes later, Bernie Coy ran up to the cell and ordered that Miller produce key 107.

"Just like I told Cretzer, you've got all my keys,

Coy. You've even got my pants. It should have been in the gallery. You've got all the keys out of the gallery, and you've got all my keys. You've got all the keys there are. You know key 107 is kept up there. You've seen it go up and down thousands of times. You've got all the keys, unless you left key 107 up in the gallery."

"Goddammit, Joe, he's right," Coy acknowledged Cretzer, now beside him in front of the cell. "Where the fuck can that key be? Go back and look again. Let's keep trying. It's gotta be there somewhere."

The initial excitement disappeared as the key crisis developed. The participants were all calm except Shockley, who continued to run back and forth in front of the cell like a disorderly child. He was wearing a gas mask and waving a wrench in one hand and a billy club in the other. He was annoying both Cretzer and Coy. Several of the D Block inmates moved quietly in and out of the isolation block, observing the activities. Also moving around but saying very little was Floyd Hamilton. Having decided he was not a player, he remained at a distance, silently observing the proceedings. Another silent observer, Ed Mrozik, drifted furtively around the periphery of the drama.

Cretzer returned to the front of the cell. "Give me your uniform jacket, Mr. Lageson," he demanded. "Shockley and Thompson want to dress up."

"Sure, Joe," Lageson responded quietly. "But you guys don't believe you can get away with this, do you?"

"Mr. Lageson, we're going and you're going with

us. At least part way, that is. Now give me the jacket." The deferential tone in Cretzer's voice was gone.

"Here, Joe. Here's my coat." Lageson tossed his uniform jacket toward Cretzer. "Think this thing through, though. You know you guys don't stand a chance. Someone's going to die. No matter who it is, your life will be over."

"Shoot him, Joe!" Shockley screamed. "Don't listen to his bullshit."

"No, Mr. Lageson, this ain't one of our bull sessions, now. This is the real thing. And we're going." Cretzer spoke with quiet resolve. "I hope you don't get hurt in this. You're a good guy, and you've got a family. But we're going, and there ain't nothing going to stop us."

Lageson took his seat on the toilet, leaned back against the wall, and sighed.

"Good try, Ernie," Bristow whispered, a weak smile on his face. "I wonder what now."

Carnes stayed in front of the cell as the other convicts busied themselves with the search for key 107. As he walked back and forth swinging his club, Carnes remarked facetiously to one of the D Block inmates standing in the doorway: "Never thought I'd end up being a cop."

12

Officer Edward Stucker had taken his detail of twenty inmates to the basement at about 1:20. In addition to the inmate barber and four prisoners receiving haircuts, his group included the clothing-room workers and those inmates scheduled for their weekly showers. By about 2:00 the first four had completed their showers, received their weekly allotment of clean clothing, and were sent by Stucker back up the stairs to be returned to their cells. At the top of the stairs they peered through the barred cage to signal the cell-house officer to open the door and pass them through to their cells.

The door between the cell house and the basement was locked at all times from the cell-house side. The key was maintained by the cell-house officer. Instead of Officer Miller, however, the returning inmates saw a group of prisoners milling around near the west end of C Block, two of whom, Cretzer and Hubbard, were holding guns. They could also see several prisoners moving about freely at the west end of the cell house. There was no sign of Officer Miller.

"Holy shit!" one of the four exclaimed, "Let's get the hell out of here. Cretzer and a bunch of guys up there are loose with guns. I don't want no part of this shit!" The others crowded in behind the lead prisoner and peeked into the cell house. Then all went back downstairs to the relative safety of the basement.

"What are you guys doing back down here?" Stucker asked, "You're supposed to go back to your cells."

"We can't get into the cell house," one of the inmates answered.

"And we don't want to, neither," another said.

The return of the four inmates attracted the attention of a number of other prisoners, and they began asking why they had come back. The four were vague, saying only that there wasn't anyone to let them into the cell house.

The way they were acting puzzled Stucker, so he went up the stairs himself to investigate. He saw a group of convicts gathered at the west end of C Block and noticed that the door to D Block was open, but he didn't see anyone with a gun. But Stucker was alarmed that neither the D Block officer nor Bill Miller were present. Rather than assume the worst, Stucker concluded that the group of prisoners he saw were probably some orderlies waiting to be passed out to the yard. But the open D Block door and the fact that no officers were visible disturbed him. He returned to the basement and called Cliff Fish in the armory to report what he had seen.

With his back to the four inmates, Stucker spoke in a whisper directly into the mouthpiece of the telephone, trying not to let the inmates know something was amiss. "Cliff, this is Ed Stucker in the basement. It looks like some kind of problem in the cell house. I just looked up there and saw seven or eight cons hanging around at the west end. I didn't recognize any of them. It doesn't look right to me. You probably ought to give Burch a call and have him check things out." Without waiting for Fish's response, Stucker hung up the phone and turned to the four inmates standing at the bottom of the stairs. "I'll get this thing squared away in a couple of minutes and you guys can go back to your cells," he assured them.

In the armory, Fish quickly dialed the west gun gallery phones, first on the cell-house side, then on the D Block side. He let each one ring five times. No answer. Confused and concerned, Fish called Stucker back.

"Ed, I get no answer on either of the gallery phones. That's pretty strange. Why don't you go back up there and take another look and I'll call the cell-house west end."

As he hung up the phone, Stucker glanced nervously around the basement. The inmates were obviously very interested.

He dashed up the stairs and looked through the

bars into the cell house. The first thing he saw was Joe Cretzer standing in front of the group of inmates, waving a pistol. Stucker stared at the gun in shocked disbelief. Suddenly Cretzer saw Stucker and came running toward the door, pointing the pistol at him. Stucker turned and raced down the stairs. He heard Cretzer yell, "There goes that son-of-a-bitch Stucker. He saw us, and he's going to turn in the alarm for sure!"

When he reached the bottom of the stairs, Stucker locked the door from the basement side with a padlock and turned to face the dozen or so convicts. If he had seen Cretzer with a pistol, he thought, probably the four inmates had seen it too and had spread the word to others in the basement. He tried to maintain his composure because he now half-expected his work details to try to join whatever was going on in the cell house, making him a hostage. Then again, he hadn't seen the gun the first time he looked out. Perhaps neither had the inmates. But he had to get word to Fish in the armory without letting the convicts in the basement overhear.

He called the armory again, but this time he dialed the emergency number, 2221. Fish answered quickly. Stucker's normally calm voice now cracked with stress.

"Cliff, Ed Stucker here," he whispered into the phone. "There is trouble in the cell house and it's goddam serious."

"What's going on, Ed?" Fish probed.

"I can't say," Stucker replied. He could not report that he had seen Joe Cretzer waving around a pistol—a .45-caliber automatic at that—obviously one of the armed guard's guns. If the men on his work details heard that, it would only be a few minutes until they overpowered him and held him hostage.

Cliff Fish quickly responded to Stucker's circumlocution. "Should I sound the siren and turn in the alarm?" he asked.

"Absolutely! Yes!" Stucker answered quickly with relief that Fish had caught on.

But Fish was feeling panicky as he hung up the phone. He had called both sides of the gun gallery, the phone in D Block, and the station at the west end of the cell house. No answer at any of them. That meant that four officers were not answering their phones. As Stucker had reported, there must be terrible trouble in the cell house. But Fish didn't want to accept responsibility for so dramatic a step as sounding the alarms.

Instead, he called the hospital, where Glen Pehrson answered the phone. "Glen, this is Cliff Fish in the armory. Is everything all right up there?"

"Sure, Cliff, everything's fine here. Why? Is there a problem somewhere?"

"Well, I don't know. I can't reach anybody in the west end of the cell house. I'm trying to find out if there's a problem."

"Well, we're okay here. Let me know if there's anything I can do to help."

"Okay, Glen, I'll get back to you if I need you."

Since Captain Weinhold was still at lunch and the associate warden was not in his office, Fish phoned the warden at home. Mrs. Johnston answered. When the armory officer asked to speak to her husband, she hesitated.

"Mr. Fish, is it really important? He's taking a nap. If you insist on talking to him, I'll wake him."

"Yes ma'am," Fish replied calmly, "I think you'd better wake him." Fish waited anxiously for what seemed an eternity, then heard the warden's formal greeting.

"Hello, Mr. Fish, this is Warden Johnston speaking. What seems to be the problem?"

"Well, Sir, I think we may have some trouble in the cell house. I'm sorry to bother you, but neither the captain nor the associate warden are here. Mr. Stucker reported from the basement that there was a problem in the cell house and suggested I call the west gun gallery. I've called both phones in the gallery, and Burch didn't answer either one. I also get no answer from the cell house or D Block phones. When he called from the basement, Stucker called in on the emergency line and said it was serious."

"It will be ten or fifteen minutes before I'll be able to be there. Do you feel we're dealing with a bad situation here?"

"Yes, Sir," the officer replied emphatically. "I think it's real bad."

"Well, Mr. Fish, if you feel the situation is bad enough, you go ahead and sound the alarm. I'll be in my office as soon as I can." With that the warden hung up, leaving Fish more confused than before.

"Shit!" he angrily exclaimed, slamming down the

phone. "So what do I do now? Goddammit, why the hell would the warden pass the buck to me?"

Looking out into the administrative offices, Fish was relieved to see Captain Weinhold return to his office. Weinhold had taken a late lunch, having been delayed in his office with correspondence. After lunch he and his wife had become involved in a detailed discussion of the upcoming birthday party for their daughter Betty. As a result, the captain was late getting back to his office.

Opening a panel in the thick, bulletproof glass wall of the armory, Fish called out to Weinhold, who had just settled in behind his desk. "Captain, we've got some kind of a problem in the cell house. Stucker just called to report that a bunch of cons are milling around the west end of the cell house. He suggested I try to reach the west gun gallery, but Burch doesn't answer his phone. I also couldn't get an answer to my calls to the cell-house west end or D Block."

Had he taken the time to analyze the situation, Captain Weinhold might have concluded that an extremely serious situation existed, requiring a cautious approach. Caution and forethought, however, were not the captain's style. In the Prussian manner for which he had become so well known on the island, ex-Marine and Captain-of-the-Guard Henry Weinhold jammed on his hat and headed for the cell house, leaving Fish stuttering, trying to relate his conversation with Warden Johnston.

Henry Weinhold was an aggressive, impulsive man who had never significantly altered his lifestyle from his Marine Corps days. His dictatorial style was not well received by the inmates. His whistle signals, which frequently controlled cell-house counts and movements, were derided and scorned by most of the inmates. He was often the target of whispered inmate threats.

Weinhold left so hurriedly that Fish had no idea when he would return or what action, if any, should be taken if he did not immediately return. "Get the associate warden as quick as you can and keep trying to raise Burch in the gun gallery!" Weinhold shouted as he left.

As Weinhold burst into the cavernous cell house, he was struck by the fact that no officers or inmates were visible. Everything was unusually quiet. He ignored the potential danger and headed directly west down Broadway, where Coy and the others had hidden themselves.

At the west end of B Block, Joe Carnes peeked around the corner, looking for any activity at the main gate or the east end of Broadway. Since he no longer had to watch for Burdett in the kitchen, he could not devote his full attention to the east end of the cell house and warn the others if anyone entered through the main gate. Yet the moment Weinhold entered the cell house, Carnes knew who it was by his erect posture and military gait.

Carnes stepped back behind the cell block so he was completely hidden. He waved his arms frantically, trying to attract Hubbard's attention without yelling.

"It's Weinhold," Carnes whispered, pointing

down Broadway. "He's coming this way, and he's alone."

Hubbard moved to the edge of Broadway, completely hidden behind C Block. He and Carnes listened carefully. The only sound in the cell house was the click of Captain Weinhold's leather heels against the concrete floor.

As Weinhold reached the end of Broadway, Hubbard stepped out to meet him face to face and pointed the rifle at his chest. "Well, we get you too?" smiled Hubbard. "Hey, Bernie, what should we do with this guy?"

"Put him in my cell," Coy said, "and get his uniform."

Hubbard prodded Weinhold in the back with the rifle and took pleasure in marching the captain into Coy's cell on the north side of B Block. "Take off your uniform, Captain. We're gonna need it more than you," he said. Hubbard took the uniform and left Carnes to stand guard in front of the open cell while Hubbard returned to the desk.

Carnes and Weinhold stared at one another. Neither man spoke. Showing off a little, Carnes began slapping the end of the club he held in his right hand against the open palm of his left hand, all the while staring without expression at the captain. But with his years of prison experience, Weinhold wasn't so easily intimidated. He returned the young Indian's stare impassively.

The impasse was ended by Coy. "Bring that dirty son of a bitch over here," Coy called out.

Carnes motioned Weinhold to come out of the

cell. Carnes jabbed him in the back with the club as he moved Weinhold, now without his trousers or jacket, to cell 404. At the west end of C Block, they were met by Cretzer and Shockley. With no warning, Shockley rushed at Weinhold and took a long, looping swing at him. Weinhold ducked the hook and took a quick step to his left. This caused Shockley to miss entirely and lurch awkwardly past the captain. As Shockley tried to catch his balance, Weinhold backhanded him across the mouth, knocking him to the floor. In a frenzy Shockley jumped to his feet and came at the captain again. Joe Cretzer stepped between them. He pointed the .45 automatic at Shockley. "Take it easy, Sam, you dumb son of a bitch," he said.

Shockley was speechless with rage and bleeding from the mouth from Weinhold's blow. But he backed off in the face of Cretzer's stern rebuke and the pistol pointed at his chest. "I want his ass, Joe. I do. I want his ass. We've got to kill that motherfucker."

"Come on over here and get in this end cell," Cretzer ordered, waving the pistol at Weinhold and ignoring Shockley. Weinhold walked into the now empty cell 404. Shockley suddenly ran up behind him and before Cretzer could intervene slugged the captain in the back of the head. Pleased with himself at last, Shockley drifted quietly away and wandered back into D Block.

As Shockley meandered off, Coy arrived out of D Block, carrying the rifle. He was upset at the sight of Weinhold in cell 404. "What's he doing in there?"

Coy asked. "Get him out of there. Put him next door with the others. I want all these guys locked in, and 404 don't lock."

"Okay, Weinhold," Cretzer ordered, "get in here with these other guys."

"Oh, for God's sake, make up your minds," Weinhold said. "Where do you want me?" Coy was now at the control box and opened cell 403. Cretzer made a show of pushing Weinhold into the cell with the other officers.

Still not intimidated by the sight of both a pistol and a rifle in the hands of his captors, Weinhold tried to point out the hopelessness of the prisoners' situation to Cretzer. "You know, you'll never get out of the cell house," he said.

"We'll get out of here, Captain. You can count on it. Just wait and see," Cretzer said.

"Even if you do get outside, you'll be killed before you get out of the yard," Weinhold said.

Before he could respond, Cretzer heard Carnes whisper from the end of C Block, "More screws coming."

13

Cliff Fish grew more and more frustrated. He still couldn't reach anybody in the cell house by telephone. He called Besk and Levinson in the Hill and Road Towers, but they both reported that everything seemed normal. Fish advised them that he was trying to locate the associate warden and requested their help in finding him and sending him "up top."

At his desk in the administrative office area, Lieutenant Simpson had been reviewing month-end reports. It had been several minutes since Weinhold stormed into the cell house, and Simpson was becoming concerned. "Have you heard from anybody in the cell house yet, Cliff? What's the status back there?"

"I don't know, Joe," Fish replied. "Captain Weinhold went in there twenty minutes ago and hasn't been heard from since. I can't raise anybody on any of the cell-house phones, but the tower guards say everything looks normal. To be honest with you, I don't know what the hell's going on back there, but I'm getting more than a little nervous."

Simpson grabbed his coat and hat and, calling to the mail clerk, Bob Baker, headed toward the cell house. "Come on, Bob, something's going on in there. Let's go help Weinhold." Baker's primary duty was to censor mail. He hadn't been following the conversation but jumped up and followed Simpson to the main gate.

"I don't think you guys ought to go in there, Joe," Fish warned. "There's got to be trouble back there, and I think you should wait till we know a little more about what's going on."

"Naw, it's probably just a fight," Simpson suggested. "We're going in to help the captain. Open the gate."

The two men headed briskly down Broadway to the west end. About halfway down the corridor, Simpson pointed to the second tier of C Block, where five or six inmates were coming downstairs from the first tier to the flats. "What's going on?" he asked, quickening his step. Both men heard a telephone ringing somewhere in the west end of the cell house, but it went unanswered.

When Simpson and Baker arrived at Times Square, they were immediately captured. Thompson now held the rifle and Cretzer the pistol. Cretzer led while Thompson and Carnes prodded Simpson and Baker from behind with the rifle and billy club. They marched around C Block, past cells 404 and 403, and into cell 402. As they passed the D Block door, Fleish and Shockley observed the new arrivals. "Ah ha, now they've got the lieutenant as well," Fleish laughed.

Seeing Baker and Simpson leave for the cell house, Carl Sundstrom decided that he, too, should do something. Before he did, though, he picked up his phone and dialed D Block. After three rings the phone was answered. Sundstrom couldn't identify the gruff voice.

"Hello."

"This is Sundstrom. What's going on back there?"

No answer.

"Who is this?"

Still no answer. A moment later the phone was hung up.

Sundstrom shook his head and hung up himself. This doesn't make sense. I wonder if there's a fight and everyone's just standing around watching it? No, that can't be. He removed a gas billy from the bottom drawer of his desk, stuck it into his back pocket, and headed for the cell house.

He passed through the main gate just a few minutes after Simpson and Baker and set out on a dead run down Broadway to the west end of the cell house. When he got within thirty feet of the end of the block, Thompson stepped out from behind C Block with the rifle in his hand. Behind him was Hubbard with a billy club in one hand and a butcher knife in the other. Shockley stepped out and shouted at Cretzer, "Hey, Joe, we got us another one!"

Sundstrom was quickly taken around C Block and into cell 402 with Simpson and Baker. As Sundstrom turned to go into the cell, Shockley ran up behind him, struck him several times with his fist on the side of the head and jaw, and shouted, "We've got you all now, you yellow-bellied bastards!"

Baker and Simpson were already sitting on the bunk, so Sundstrom moved to the rear of the cell and leaned against the back wall. The three men stared morosely at one another. None of them spoke.

In a few minutes, Cretzer returned to the front of the cell and demanded that Sundstrom remove his pants. As he did, the gas billy fell out of his pocket and clattered on the floor. Cretzer heard the sound but ignored it. He was more concerned with getting the uniform. As Sundstrom handed his trousers to Cretzer, his wallet fell out and landed on the floor near the front of the cell. Cretzer picked it up and removed all the cash. Counting the currency, Cretzer handed the billfold back. "Hmm, ninety-two dollars. Not bad. We can use this when we get to Frisco. Just call it highway robbery, Sundstrom," Cretzer said. He laughed as he tucked the bills into his pocket.

Taking the pants and money, Cretzer disappeared around the corner of the block, leaving only Shockley at the front of the cells. Sundstrom returned to the back of the cell where he found a pair of prison dungarees to replace his confiscated uniform pants.

As the last four officers entered the cell house and were captured, Ernie Lageson was straining to hear the conversation among the inmates coming from the area of the yard door and the cell-house officer's desk. Someone had brought a ladder from the kitchen and propped it against the bars of the gun gallery in Times Square. They still hadn't been able to find the yard-door key. Lageson could hear snatches of the conversation between Coy and Cretzer as they picked through the keys. Thompson had been trying all the keys in the lock without success.

"Bernie, Frisco's as far away as it ever was. We're not getting out of this fucking hole. We're trapped," Cretzer said.

Thompson continued trying one key after another. When he had gone through all of them, he started again, mumbling all the while. Ernie Lageson smiled, then chuckled to himself. What Thompson and the others didn't realize was that by forcing the wrong key into the mechanism, they were destroying the lock. The lock was designed so that if the wrong key was used, the tumblers would bend and become distorted.

Cretzer suddenly reappeared in front of the cell. Lageson could see that he was discouraged. Looking to the upper tiers, Cretzer shouted to inmate Rudolph Brandt, "Hey Rudy, you still think you want to go along on this trip? We talked about it once. You're pretty old, though, and it's getting rough down here. But you're welcome if you want to join us." If Brandt answered, nobody could hear him.

Cretzer stood in front of the cell, gazing at the automatic pistol in his hand. We came so close, he thought. Despite all the activity around him, he suddenly felt alone. It was a familiar feeling. Most of what he had accomplished in life he had done alone. He had become Public Enemy Number Five, and he had done it pretty much on his own. He had not been on his own here, but, for whatever reason, it was obvious the blastout wasn't going to happen. All their planning, all that work, for nothing. They had come so close. They had the guns, they controlled the cell house, and they were the turn of a key from controlling the entire island. But it was over. They would never get out of the cell house. Stucker had seen Cretzer with a gun. That and all the unanswered telephones, the unexplained disappearance of four officers. Soon the alarm would sound. The siren would be followed by the screws and their riot guns.

What now? What were his choices? He could pick up the phone, make a surrender call, and accept the consequences. Even though they had hostages, there was no way they could make a favorable deal. Apparently Burch was alive, so there would be no death penalty. But another twenty-five to life on top of his sentences would keep him in jail the rest of his life. He would probably spend most of it in isolation and end up like Stroud. He couldn't bear to live like that. He'd rather die. (Well, he could always go out with a bang.) Fight to the death and take as many screws with him as he could. He took a deep breath. He didn't know what the others would choose, but as long as he had the pistol and at least one bullet, he would continue to fight.

Noting Cretzer's obvious dismay, Ernie Lageson

decided this might be a good time to start talking. Cretzer's emotions were no longer controlling his behavior. Before he could think what to say, though, Lageson heard the firm voice of Captain Weinhold.

Weinhold stood boldly in front of Cretzer in his underwear, vest, and neatly appointed shirt and tie. He spoke calmly. "Joe, you know you can't get out of the cell house. Even if you did, you'd never get out of the yard. A lot of people would get hurt."

"You mean killed, Captain. You mean killed," Cretzer said.

"Well, maybe so," Weinhold said. "The point is, you can't make it. Nobody ever has. Nobody ever will. You know that, Joe. The best thing for you to do is to hand over that gun and call this thing off. Nobody's been hurt so far. You can end this thing right now so that no one will be."

Standing behind Cretzer, Shockley overheard the conversation and immediately joined in. He looked like a clown, wearing an officer's uniform jacket several sizes too big for him. "Kill them, Joe! Kill all those yellow-bellied bastards. Don't listen to that horseshit. Kill them, Joe!"

Thompson, standing nearby, joined in. "Yeah, Joe, shut him up."

The captain's calm manner and firm voice remained unaffected. He continued talking in an unemotional tone, his voice resolute and unyielding. "You're too smart to listen to that fool Shockley, Joe. Think about it. You know this thing's not going anywhere. The alarm will sound soon, and it'll be all over."

As he stood at the west end of C Block staring at the pile of keys, Coy was also coming to grips with the reality of the situation. Yet he wasn't as fatalistic as Cretzer. This was his plan. He had conceived it. He had developed it. He had brought it this far, and he wouldn't let it die without a fight. The key to the yard door wasn't available, so that part of the plan would have to be abandoned. At one time he had considered going through a skylight in the roof and capturing the weapons in the Main Tower. He had discarded that idea in favor of key 107 and the yard door, but now he would reactivate the original plan and try to make it work.

That plan required the large, rolling scaffold used for changing light bulbs in the overhead fixtures. It was kept on Seedy Street near the library. The scaffold contained extension ladders that could reach to the ceiling. Using the ladders to break through the skylight in the roof, they could attack the Main Tower with their weapons and get more guns. From there they could go down the side of the cell house and make their way to the dock. The plan was risky because Coy didn't know how easy it would be to get through the skylight. He also didn't know where the Main Tower guard would be, so there was no certainty of surprising the guard. But there wasn't any choice now.

Coy called to Carnes and Thompson. "Wheel that scaffolding over to the west end, boys." They ran to the scaffold and began pushing it up Seedy Street. As he waited, Coy began to feel the same excitement he had experienced just before he scaled the gun gallery earlier in the afternoon. I'll make it work, he thought to himself. I've come too far. I can't fail now. "Come on, you guys, hurry up!" he shouted. "Get that thing up here!"

14

In the armory, Cliff Fish had been phoning at a frantic pace. Warden Johnston still had not arrived. Fish gave up on contacting anyone in the cell house and began calling every outlying duty station, including second calls to Besk and Levinson. Both men reported that everything in their area still appeared normal. Both men assured Fish that they would immediately report anything out of the ordinary. He received the same responses from Jim Comerford in the Dock Tower and John Barker on the yard wall, as well as from the Model Shop, Powerhouse and Main Towers.

Ike Faulk, the lieutenant in charge of the dock, was not satisfied with Fish's report of "trouble in the cell house" and demanded more detail.

"I can't give you any details, Ike. All I know is I'm not getting any response from D Block, the west gun gallery, or the cell house. Pehrson reports every-thing's normal in the hospital. Stucker was the guy who turned in the initial alarm, but all he reported was trouble in the cell house."

"Is there anybody in the east gun gallery?" in-quired Faulk. "Has it been manned yet?"

"I don't know. I don't think so," Fish said. "When I told Weinhold about the problem, he ran right into the cell house but didn't do anything about manning the east gallery."

"Well, it sounds to me like you need help up there. I'm coming up. Get some rifles and riot guns ready. We've got to get somebody into the east gallery and see if we can't find out what the hell's going on in there. Has either the associate warden or the warden been notified yet?"

"I called the warden, but I can't find Miller. Have you seen him?"

"Yeah, he was here just a few minutes ago and headed down toward the powerhouse. He was do-ing a north-island inspection, I think."

"Well, maybe someone will send him up here," Fish remarked hopefully. "I've called all the towers and duty stations up there and told everyone to be on the lookout for him."

"Cliff, I think you should sound the alarm. I don't know whether that's my call or not, but I'll accept the responsibility. Go ahead and activate the siren and the powerhouse whistle. I'll grab one of the trucks and be right up there."

"Okay, Ike, see you soon, and thanks." Fish hung up the phone, more at ease now that someone had finally taken command. Fish threw the switches that activated the escape siren and the steam whistle located at the powerhouse. He smiled as he listened to the chorus of the whistle and the rising whine of the siren.

Back in the cell house, Carnes and Thompson had moved the scaffold only a few feet when the escape siren begin to wail. It started slowly, and built rapidly. Within seconds it reached a screaming pitch that could be heard as far as San Francisco and Marin County.

Coy's exuberance immediately deflated. There was no hope now. No hope at all of getting out of the cell house. Every gun on the island would be trained on the cell house. Every off-duty officer would be back on duty with a gun in his hand. The entire island would be on armed alert. Coy picked up the rifle. He grabbed the belt with the ammunition pouches and threw it over his shoulder.

Looking down Seedy Street, he saw that Carnes and Thompson had discarded the scaffold and joined Joe Cretzer in front of cells 402 and 403. The D Block inmates had all disappeared when the siren sounded. Franklin was still locked in D Block isolation. Hamilton had chosen not to go. Mrozik was no place to be found, and Coy didn't know how long Carnes and Thompson would hang on. He waved to Hubbard and Carnes and called out, "Come on you guys, let's go get us some tower screws!" As he walked by the yard door, he looked sadly at the pile of keys and shook his head. "If only we'd found that fucking key 107," Coy said.

Lieutenant Faulk fired up one of the aging work trucks, rumbled across the open dock area, and started up the steep road to the top level of the island. The road from the dock to the top zigzagged back and forth like an alpine highway and had three hairpin curves of 180 degrees. Faulk was about to make the third of these when he caught sight of the associate warden lumbering toward him. He stopped the truck as the overweight Miller arrived, perspiring profusely and breathing heavily. The whine of the siren was deafening. The two men had to shout to be heard.

"There's some kind of a problem in the cell house, Ed!" shouted Faulk as Miller approached.

"Yeah, I know. I talked to Besk, and I'm on my way up there now. Why don't you head back to the dock and send whatever men you can spare up top."

"Okay," replied Faulk. "I'll send everybody up and handle things down there by myself. I'll move the cons up to the Hill Tower sally port, and then my officers can head up top. Fish tells me there's nobody in the east gun gallery. That should've been manned at the first sign of trouble."

"Right, Ike. I'll take care of that first thing when I get up there," Miller said. "See you later." As Faulk turned the vehicle around to return to the dock, Miller continued his laborious climb to the top of the island.

The scream of the siren created tense excitement throughout the work area. To caged men, the sound of an escape alarm was exhilarating. Every convict hoped the escapee would be successful. The guards, of course, immediately went on alert to control the situation and prevent sympathetic demonstrations or other unruly activity. In the shops and work stations around the island, wild-eyed prisoners stood motionless, listening to the seldom-heard, dramatic sound. The men guarding them tensed, more alert than ever.

But to the prisoners in the cell house, the sound of the siren meant an end rather than a beginning. Now there was no chance at all of escape. Their well-planned escape attempt would degenerate into a simple prison riot. Coy hit the wall with his fist angrily. "Shit, Joe, we took control of the cell house. We got ten guards for hostages. We were almost there!" he said.

"Yeah, but that fucking key."

"I know," Coy interrupted. "Where the fuck could it have gone?"

"Well, it doesn't matter now. Not at all." Cretzer said.

Immediately after the siren sounded, all the D Block inmates except Shockley returned to the isolation cells. Many of the inmates doubled up or formed groups to help one another during the hours ahead. They moved mattresses, pillows, blankets, and other items to the front of the cells, creating protective walls to shield themselves from the anticipated gunfire and tear gas.

With Hubbard at his side and Carnes tagging along behind, Coy strode through the dining hall and burst into the kitchen past the cowering kitchen workers. On the north side of the kitchen, he used the rifle butt to smash out one of the windows. That gave him a clear view of the Dock Tower. He rested the rifle on the windowsill and carefully sighted in on Dock Tower Officer Jim Comerford. Coy fired twice. Comerford had been scanning the windows of the cell house when the shots rang out. He collapsed motionless on the tower deck.

"You got him, Bernie. Nice shot!" Hubbard said, slapping Coy on the shoulder. They stood for a moment studying the motionless form on the tower deck and concluded he was dead.

"Let's go to the bake shop," Coy said. "We'll nail the son of a bitch in the Hill Tower."

Carnes protested weakly. "Hey, Bernie, what good is that gonna do?"

Coy, Hubbard, and Carnes crossed the kitchen and moved into the bakery. Coy again smashed out a pane of glass, sighted with care, and fired twice, this time at the Hill Tower. Besk, standing on the tower catwalk, spun around and dropped where he stood. The officer appeared lifeless, his rifle still leaning against the rail. Hubbard could barely contain himself. "You got him too, Bernie. You nailed them both. Let's go get the guy in the Road Tower."

As Hubbard and Coy moved to the windows facing the Road Tower, Carnes walked slowly out of the kitchen and into the dining hall. He sat at one of the tables, brooding, not knowing what to do next.

Moving back into the kitchen, this time to the south wall, Coy went through the same procedure, firing two shots at Irving Levinson in the Road Tower. Levinson was standing outside the tower enclosure and went down in a motionless heap. Triumphant with their success, Hubbard and Coy returned to the dining hall and headed back to the cell house.

As the siren blared, Captain Weinhold got Joe Cretzer's attention and started again. "There it is, Joe, the alarm. You'll never get out that door now."

Sam Shockley began to panic at the sound of the alarm. He stood behind Cretzer holding a large pipe wrench. "Don't listen to him, Joe. Kill him. Let's kill every goddam one of 'em. Don't leave no witnesses."

Cretzer ignored Shockley, and locked stares with Weinhold. The captain continued talking in a calm voice as Cretzer listened silently.

Just then, Buddy Thompson arrived in front of the cell. "I'm with Sam, Joe. Let's kill them."

"Listen, Joe," Weinhold continued. "Don't pay any attention to those guys. Why don't you get Coy over here and let me talk to him. Look at it this way, Joe. With the alarm sounding and the whole island on alert, you know now you can never get out of the cell house. Even if you get that door open, the first man to step out is going to be the first man to die."

Cretzer finally snapped. His face twisted in rage and frustration. He raised the .45 automatic dramatically. "No, Captain, you'll be the first to die."

"Well, you can only die once," Weinhold replied.

Cretzer fired. The huge pistol roared, sending a bullet completely through Weinhold's body and knocking him to the floor. In a frenzy, Cretzer fired shot after shot into the cell full of officers. Corwin was hit in the face and crumpled in the right rear corner of the cell. Miller, seated on the bunk, took a shot that went through his chest and arm. Everybody in the cell dived, ducked, or fell in an effort to avoid being hit.

After firing several rounds into cell 403, Cretzer moved to cell 402, where he shot Simpson in the chest and then shot Baker. He fired at Sundstrom, who dived to the floor in the back of the cell. The thunder of the heavy pistol and the whining ricochet of the bullets temporarily drowned out the sound of the siren.

Then, as suddenly as it had begun, the shooting was over. The only sound was the siren. Swirling blue-gray smoke drifted up from the front of the cells. Cretzer stood silently staring into the cells and at the bodies covering the floors. He had just gunned down nine men in cold blood, and it hadn't changed a thing. They were still trapped in the cell house. Frisco was still just as far away as ever. His shoulders fell. The gun hung at his side as Cretzer turned and walked slowly past cell 403 toward the west end of the cell house and the locked outside door.

Suddenly Shockley began screaming again. "Hey, Joe, there's a son of a bitch in the corner there that's still alive. Kill him."

"Yeah, Joe, kill him. We don't want to leave no witnesses," Thompson said.

Cretzer peered into the dimness of the rear of cell 403 and saw Ernie Lageson sitting calmly on the toilet, looking straight ahead. "That's Mr. Lageson," he said. "He's my friend. He's a good screw and always treated me right."

"Friend? Hell!" protested Thompson. "He'll testify against us, go to court, and fuck us all. Kill him! We don't want no witnesses."

Ernie felt an eerie calmness replace the sick fear he had been feeling. He knew he was about to die. "Please, God, look after Eunice and Little Ern," he prayed. "And please let this be quick."

Now Cretzer felt like he had no choice but to shoot Lageson. If he didn't, Thompson would for sure. Yet as he looked at the man he considered a friend, he didn't want him to die. There was no reason for it. He rested the barrel of the pistol on the crossbar and pointed it at Ernie. "Mr. Lageson, I'm really sorry about this," Cretzer said. He pulled the trigger. The hammer clicked harmlessly. The gun was empty.

The click was more startling to Lageson than a gunshot would have been. Everyone watched Cretzer. He ejected the spent clip, rammed in a fresh clip of seven bullets, and again pulled the slide back on the .45 automatic, cocking it. As he reloaded, Cretzer couldn't take his eyes off his friend sitting in the corner of the cell. There would never be a trial for Cretzer; Lageson would never testify against him. Joe Cretzer was going out fighting. As the two men stared into one another's eyes, Cretzer thought again, there's no reason for this man to die. He rested the barrel on the crossbar once again, pointed the gun at Lageson, and tightened his grip on the pistol. As he applied the final pressure to the trigger, he moved the barrel imperceptibly to the right and squeezed. There was another booming explosion as the gun fired. Lageson pitched forward, his head between his legs.

"Be sure you got these guys," urged Shockley pointing to the motionless bodies of Simpson, Baker, and Sundstrom. Stepping back to cell 402, Cretzer fired once more at Simpson and Baker. Both bodies bounced from the impact of the giant pistol slugs, then did not move. After all this, Cretzer was calm. The sharp, acrid odor of gunpowder lingered in the air. The cell house was again quiet. Outside the siren continued to wail.

Associate Warden Miller struggled up the steep roadway to the entrance of the huge yellow prison building and burst into the administration offices. "What's going on, Cliff?" he demanded of the armory officer.

"We really don't know, Ed. I can't raise anybody on the phones in the cell house. The Captain, Lieutenant Simpson, Baker, and Sundstrom all went in over the past twenty minutes. We haven't heard from any of them. The only report I received was a couple of cryptic phone calls from Stucker in the basement reporting that there was trouble in the cell house. He didn't say what the trouble was. The towers all report everything normal."

"Give me a gas billy, Cliff. I'm going in there. Notify the warden and get every off-duty officer up here as soon as they can get here. Send the first two

men who report into the east gun gallery and arm
them with rifles and riot guns." Turning away from
the armory, Miller called to Phillips. "Let me in there,
Lloyd." Ignoring prison regulations, Phillips and Fish
threw open all the sections of the main gate at once
and passed the associate warden into the cell house.
Without hesitation, still nearly out of breath, Miller
charged down Broadway toward the west end of the
cell house.

Coy and Hubbard walked briskly through the
dining room back to the cell house. Hubbard was
still congratulating Coy on his sharp shooting. Carnes
trudged behind them. Carnes was now really worried. He was young, after all, and could do plenty of
time and still get out to have some kind of life. But
by killing the guards, Coy had executed him, too. He
idolized Coy, but was beginning to hate him as well.

As they approached the cell-house door, the
three men were startled to see the familiar figure of
Associate Warden Miller charging at them down
Broadway. He carried a club in his right hand and
was running faster than any of them had ever seen
him move. "Give me the gun," pleaded Hubbard. "I
want that Jughead son of a bitch." He took the gun
from Coy, concealed it behind his back, and walked
quickly out of the dining hall and several feet into
Times Square. As Miller got closer, Hubbard pulled
out the rifle and aimed at the corpulent figure running toward him. "Die, you son of a bitch," Hubbard
said quietly as he pulled the trigger. At the exact
moment he fired, Hubbard was bumped from behind by Carnes. The gun barrel flew up, sending the

bullet impotently into the ceiling. Furious, Hubbard spun around to face the hapless Carnes.

"Jeez, Marv, I'm sorry. I didn't know you were going to stop so sudden," Carnes said.

Seeing the gun, Miller tried to change direction, lost his balance, and fell to one knee. He scrambled to his feet and began running in the opposite direction. He headed back to the main gate and shouted to Phillips to open the gate. At the same time, he activated the gas billy and tried to throw it over his shoulder. His aim was wild. The billy hit the underside of the cell overhang and exploded in his face. Miller was partially blinded by the blast, but he made it back to the main gate.

The confusion that was once confined to the armory now spread to the administrative offices. The warden finally arrived and demanded a full briefing from Miller, who was still in the cell house. When he returned to the administrative offices a few moments later, Miller was in no condition to report to anyone. His face was badly burned, and he was still partially blinded by the gas-billy blast. Loring Mills, the warden's administrative assistant, found a first-aid kit and began trying to treat the injured Miller. Hearing Miller's voice, the warden emerged from his office and began to question his second-in-command as to conditions inside the prison.

"I don't know for sure what's going on in there, Warden, but I do know the convicts are loose and they've got a gun. I can only assume they somehow got into the west gun gallery and got Burch's weapons. That means they have a rifle and a pistol. As I went down Broadway, I saw Coy with a rifle. He took a couple of shots at me." Under the stress of the situation, Miller formed the opinion that Coy had wielded the rifle and fired at him. "There were others there, but I didn't have enough time to identify them. I didn't see any officers, so I have no idea whether they're alive or dead."

Running a quick count in his mind, Miller further advised the warden, "There are ten officers in there unaccounted for. I've made arrangements to have all the inmates mustered in the industrial area and moved into the yard. Extra men will be assigned to the yard wall. I think one of our first considerations should be to put a team together and go into the cell house and bring out those captured officers. Before that, though, we should make an effort at getting the prisoners to surrender. The problem now is, we don't know for sure where they are or what they have in mind. I've ordered the east gun gallery manned, and the men up there will be able to give us a good description of what's going on in the cell house and how many prisoners are involved. The prisoners have the keys to get themselves out into the yard, but for some reason so far they haven't tried to leave the cell house. The first thing to do is to get all the off-duty men up here, station them around the cell house to prevent any breach of the building's perimeter, and then plan our attack."

"Well, Ed, I don't want anyone going into the cell house until we know a whole lot more about things than we know now," the warden said. "We don't know where the convicts are, how many are involved, or how well armed they are. I think it is imperative that we locate them geographically within the cell house. I don't want any weapons going in there if there is the least possible chance they may fall into the hands of the inmates. Now you better get that face of yours taken care of. Given the circumstances, I think we should call for help from other agencies. I should send a telegram to the press. I'll make the necessary calls. You keep me advised."

15

With the siren turned off, the cell house was once again quiet. Except for Coy, Cretzer, Hubbard, Thompson, and Carnes, the corridors were deserted.

Soon after the last shot was fired, Sam Shockley had taken off the baggy guard's jacket he had been wearing, tossed the pipe wrench into the C Block utility corridor, and slipped unnoticed back into D Block. He climbed the stairs to the second tier and joined Ed Sharp, Jack Pepper, Jim Quillan, and Howard Butler, who were piling mattresses and blankets in the front of one of the cells as a barrier. Shockley was still wild-eyed and mumbling to himself; he appeared to the others to be in a trance. The men were accustomed to watching as Shockley hallucinated, heard voices, and received phantom messages from alien beings, so no one took particular

notice of his appearance or conduct. As he entered
the cell, he drew his right index finger across his
throat, but didn't say anything. The men made a
space for him on the floor.

"How's it going?" one of them asked.

"Pretty good, pretty good," Shockley responded.
"But I think some guys got shot."

"Well, we're okay," Sharp announced cheerfully.
"Let's get as many mattresses in here as we can. It's
my guess that those fucking screws are gonna start
shooting this place up pretty soon. Where's Coy and
Cretzer and the other guys, Sam?"

"I don't know," Shockley responded. "They was
all down working on the door, trying to get out into
the yard, but none of the keys worked. It was fun
while it lasted, though."

In cell 403 Ernie Lageson fought through a haze
of semiconsciousness. Gradually he revived but was
disoriented and confused as to his surroundings. As
he awoke, the pain hit him. Then he realized where
he was. I should be dead! The vivid image of Cretzer
apologizing as he pulled the trigger flashed in Ernie's
mind. Without changing his position, he listened for
any sound from the corridor in front of the cell.
Hearing nothing, he cautiously lifted his head
enough to see the front of the cell. No one was out
there. He saw no sign of life in the cell. He heard
voices in the distance but couldn't understand what
was being said, nor could he identify the speakers.
He began to feel detached, as if he were floating. He

had trouble concentrating. Ernie slipped back into unconsciousness.

Eventually his mind began to clear. Ernie realized he was still seated on the toilet with his head pitched forward between his legs. This time he could locate the pain, a blinding pain on the left side of his head. He wondered how much of his face had been torn away. Slowly he moved his hand to his cheek, almost afraid of what he would find. He carefully ran his fingers over the wound. His face was numb and badly swollen but seemed intact. He had been hit on the cheek. Blood was still streaming from the wound. There was a small pool of blood on the floor and blood all over his fingers. Again he thought, I should be dead. How had Cretzer missed from that short distance? He was only five feet away when he fired.

Lageson heard the sound of footsteps approaching the cell. He froze and held his breath. Out of the corner of his eye, he saw a shadowy figure at the front of the cell. The individual lingered, then moved slowly on to the next cell, then returned to the front of cell 403. It's one of the cons, Lageson thought, probably checking to make sure we're all dead. After what seemed an eternity, the shadow turned and walked back to the west end of the cell house.

Guessing that the area in front of the cell was now deserted, Lageson again moved slightly to his left and raised his head just enough to get a complete view of the cell.

Captain Weinhold was slumped by the door, his legs across the front of the cell and his head down on his chest. Bristow lay under the bunk. Burdett was sprawled across the bunk, partially on and partially off, with his head hanging over the side. Miller lay crumpled on the bunk. Looking to his left, he saw Corwin in a seated position on the floor in the rear of the cell. His appearance was grotesque. The lower half of his face was distorted and covered with blood. It appeared he had been shot in the face. Lageson saw no sign of life and assumed he was the only one in the cell still alive. His head throbbed with pain, but he knew that the wound was not life threatening, perhaps not even serious.

At the west end of the cell house, by the door to the yard, Buddy Thompson continued trying different keys in the door. Joe Cretzer still held the pistol. Coy held the rifle. They stood quietly, looking on. The tower guards were dead, shot by Coy with the rifle. If they could get through the yard door, there was nothing to stop them from continuing the break, despite the siren. Neither of them spoke. Coy and Cretzer were very subdued.

Hubbard, though, was still running on adrenalin. "Hey, Kid," he said to Joe Carnes, "go check and be sure that the screws are all dead. If they're not, use this." He removed the butcher knife from his belt and held it out to the young man.

But Carnes was rapidly losing interest in the entire affair. He did as he was told, returned to the hostage cells, and peered in apathetically. He had no intention of entering the cells and using the knife.

He simply glanced into the cells, then returned to make his report to the others. "The cocksuckers are all dead. They're just the way we left them," he said.

Ernie Lageson rose up slightly and studied his wounded companions with greater care. Weinhold's chest was moving, so it was obvious he was alive, but his breathing seemed shallow and labored. Corwin was breathing. So was Miller. Bristow was out of sight, but Burdett was sprawled across the bunk, his head near Lageson. Moving as close to Burdett as he could, Lageson whispered, "Are you okay, Joe?"

"Yeah, Ernie, I'm fine," Burdett whispered. "What about the others?"

"Everybody's alive, but Weinhold, Miller, and Corwin are shot bad. I don't know about Bristow."

"I'm okay," the chief steward said from under the bunk.

"Come on, Marv," Coy said. "Let's climb up C Block and see if we can do anything at the roof. Maybe we can still get out through the vents or skylights and take a shot at the Main Tower. There's a tommy gun up there, you know."

Coy entered the open door to the C Block utility corridor and climbed aloft through the maze of pipes and conduits. Hubbard followed closely behind. Carnes tagged along, there being nothing else for him to do. It was not an easy climb, but all three men were in excellent physical condition, and they made the climb with relative ease.

Crawling out onto the top of the cell block, Coy headed for one of the large ventilators mounted on the roof. To his dismay, he found that it was constructed of heavy-gauge steel with massive bolts holding it in place. "Shit!" Coy shouted.

He turned to the skylights. He quickly found that the heavy glass was constructed with inlaid wire. To leave the cell house through the skylight would involve smashing the glass, assuming it was breakable, then cutting the wire fused inside. It would be a difficult task even with the proper tools and would create so much noise that the Main Tower officer would cut them down before they could get through the opening.

Looking over the cell house from the top of the block, Coy made one positive observation. "This is a good spot to shoot from. We've got a good line on Broadway, the main gate, and Seedy Street. When they try to rush the place, we can get us a few screws from up here."

That was twice now Carnes had heard that the others expected to die in a shoot-out. A shoot-out to the death was not what Carnes had envisioned when he threw in with Coy. Now it appeared that was all that was possible. Grasping at any other possible solution, Carnes raised a subject so often discussed throughout the prison. "Hey, Bernie, what about the tunnel to the dock that you talked about. Can't we use that? You talked a lot about that tunnel and how it came out down by the dock."

"Sorry, Old Man, there ain't no tunnel. That's just jailhouse bullshit. It looks like we're pretty well fucked now, except for taking out as many screws as we can." As he spoke, Coy saw the fear and despair in Carnes's eyes and felt a strange sense of paternal responsibility. He had brought the kid into this, after all. "Look, Old Man, I'm sorry I got you into this thing. I really thought it was going to work and I would be doing you a favor. And it almost did work. Everything worked, except we couldn't find the fucking key to the yard."

"I'm sorry, too!" Carnes snapped back. "I'm going back to my cell." As he spoke, Carnes dropped to his knees and slipped over the edge of the cell block.

"Look, no hard feelings, okay? You're young, Kid, and can do your time. Not me. I killed those tower screws, so it's the Green Room at San Quentin for me. Me and Marv and Joe, we're going down hard. You might as well cut out. There ain't even enough guns to go around now. Hey, Kid, I'm really sorry," Coy said.

"Okay, Bernie," Carnes answered sadly, his anger quickly dissipating. "Good luck." He dropped effortlessly into the darkness of the utility corridor and returned quietly to his cell.

After one final look around, Coy and Hubbard also climbed down. "Come on, Marv, let's go find Joe and see how much ammo we've got and where we want to hole up."

As they emerged from the utility corridor, Hubbard and Coy saw Carnes disappear around the end of B Block, heading for his cell. Cretzer was seated at the cell-house desk. Thompson stood leaning against the wall beside him. "The kid's cutting out, huh?" Cretzer asked with an air of resignation. "I'm not surprised." Shifting his weight from one foot to the other, Thompson wanted nothing more than to hide out in his cell, too, but was afraid to say it.

"How many rounds we got for the rifle?" Coy asked, picking up the gun belt and fumbling with the ammunition pouches. "I've got a few shells here in my pocket." He swept the remaining few keys from the top of the desk and spread out the remaining rifle ammunition. Carefully counting them, he announced, "Looks like we got twenty-two shells here. How much you got left for the pistol, Joe?"

"There's four in the gun, and I got another clip of seven in my pocket. That's eleven dead screws if we make them all count," Cretzer said. "Where are we going to hole up?"

I know where I want to hole up, Thompson thought. He risked saying it aloud. "Hey, look, you guys, with only two guns there really ain't much I can add to this thing. We ain't going anywhere, so I'm going back to my cell."

"Okay, chickenshit," Cretzer said, without looking up at Thompson.

Coy and Hubbard remained silent. Neither of them were willing to be critical of Thompson, who was simply choosing to try to stay alive rather than die. It was the end of the road. Each man had to handle it his own way. "Hey, Joe, why are you so pissed off? Let him go. Who gives a shit?" Coy finally said.

"Are Weinhold and Lageson and all of them dead?" Hubbard asked.

"I think so. I checked them. Nobody's moved," Cretzer said.

"I'm going up on C Block and see if I can nail another screw," Coy said, as he scooped up the rifle and ammunition belt.

Coy climbed the stairs to the top tier, walked to the east end, and studied the scene outside. He saw several boats lying off the island, including the prison launch. Maybe the newspapers are out there taking pictures and writing stories. We'll for sure be in tonight's papers. He also saw activity on the hill below. Guards were setting up in firing positions. He carefully scanned the landscape and the stairs leading up from the civilian area below. Coy cradled the rifle, searching for another target.

16

Dock Tower Officer Jim Comerford's wife Monica was enjoying an early afternoon cup of coffee, having put two-year-old Jeannie down for her afternoon nap. It was her first quiet period of the day, and the busy young mother welcomed the rest. Four-year-old Mary Alice was playing with some of her friends on the windswept parade ground. "Monnie" Comerford kept a casual eye on the youngsters through her kitchen window.

The parade ground on Alcatraz Island was the safest playground in the Bay Area. No traffic. No animals. No strangers. All the children were known personally by all the island adults. There were about 200 voluntary Alcatraz residents. They were like a large family. The adults always looked out for the children, whether on the island or in town. Monnie wasn't concerned, then, when she glanced out the window and didn't see the children. They must have drifted over to the little parade ground, she thought. This was a smaller open area near Building 64.

The Comerfords had moved west from New Jersey not long after Alcatraz opened as a federal prison. Like Ernie Lageson, Jim Comerford expected to be helping to rehabilitate hardened prisoners. Like Ernie—like several of the better-educated guards, for that matter—he viewed his new job as a challenge and an opportunity. Monnie was an employee of Metropolitan Life Insurance Company. She had worked there since she was fifteen. She had been able to manage a transfer and stay with the company in San Francisco. She was now in the second year of a leave of absence while she devoted all her time to making a home for her husband and three young daughters. Because of Comerford's seniority, he and his family lived in C Building, the newest dependent apartment house on the island.

The quiet calm of the early afternoon was suddenly broken by the blast of the powerhouse steam whistle, followed by the whine of the escape siren. It was a frightening sound. Although Monnie had heard it before, the siren made her shudder with shock. She felt a stab of fear. The Alcatraz dependents were under constant stress living on the penal island. The escape siren always heightened the stress. She dashed back to the kitchen window and scanned the empty parade ground. She began to panic now, with her daughter and the other children out of sight. I have to get to Mary Alice, Monnie thought. She'll be terrified.

Monnie raced down the stairs and out onto the parade ground. She ran as fast as she could in her house slippers, calling out to her daughter. She couldn't find the children. She headed for the little parade ground, hoping to find them at the popular play area. On windy days the children often played there because it was more sheltered than the larger open area. When she was halfway across the parade ground, she heard a blast of gunfire coming from the cell house. Her heart froze. She had never heard the sound of gunfire on Alcatraz. "Oh, my God," she yelled. Where are they? There was no sign of the children on the little parade ground.

On the east side of the old army parade ground, she ran down the stairs to the lower balcony of Building 64. It ran along the north and east sides of the larger apartment house. She was now frantically shouting her daughter's name. "Mary Alice! Mary Alice! Where are you?"

"Monnie! Monnie! She's okay! They're up in the Stites's apartment. They're all okay," Irene Bristow called from her apartment window. "The kids are fine, but your Jim's been shot! He's lying on the floor of the tower, and he's not moving. From down here you can't tell how bad it is. Go up on the upper balcony and see how he is. Be careful, though, someone's shooting from the cell house."

"Oh, no!" Monnie cried hysterically. She ran into the building and climbed the stairs to the upper balcony. The upper balcony was at the same level as the floor of the Dock Tower, exposed to the north end of the island but not visible from the cell house.

Monnie ran the length of the balcony, staying close to the wall of the building until she was directly across from the tower and the prostrate body of her husband. He was lying on the outside deck, behind the tower enclosure.

"Jim! Jim! Are you all right?"

"I'm okay, Monnie," Comerford shouted back, without moving. "Whoever was shooting missed me. I'm safe where I am now, but I'm not going to move. If they start shooting again, I'll use this," he said, referring to the Thompson submachine gun he held in his arms. "Don't worry about me. I'll be fine. Get back inside and take care of the girls. I'm okay."

At about 3:20, Officer Hershel Oldham awoke from his afternoon nap in the bachelor officers' quarters adjacent to the dock. He worked the evening watch from four until midnight, and it was the beginning of the day for him. He pulled on his uniform and headed to the cell house for an early supper before going on duty. As he passed the dock office, Lieutenant Emil Rychner, who had relieved Faulk as dock officer, called out to him and inquired as to where he had been.

"I've been asleep, Rych," Oldham said.

"Jesus Christ, you are one sound sleeper!" Rychner said. "The escape siren and whistle from the powerhouse blasted away for what seemed like forever, and you didn't hear a thing? Nobody could have slept through that."

"Escape?" Oldham repeated. "What's going on?"

"Serious trouble up top," Rychner said. "Somebody took a shot at Comerford. The report is that the cons are loose in the cell house with guns. I suggest you get your ass up top pronto. Go by way of the parade ground and the east side of the island. There's been shooting from the north and west sides of the cell house, so keep your eyes open. If you can see them, they can see you."

Looking up at the Dock Tower above him, Oldham saw the motionless body of Comerford lying on the tower deck. "Is Jim okay?" Oldham asked. "He's not moving."

"Yeah, he's fine. They missed him. He called down that he's okay, but he's playing possum up there so they don't shoot again. He also slid around, so he's behind the glass wall now," explained Rychner.

"How about the guys in the cell house—Miller, Lageson, and the others? Are they okay?" Oldham asked.

"Nobody knows," the lieutenant said.

Heeding Rychner's advice, Oldham took the circuitous route to the top. He mounted the long flight of stairs from the dock to Building 64, then climbed more stairs to the parade ground. He crossed the open expanse of cement and finally reached the outer-perimeter security fence. He let himself through the locked gate and ran along the steep road leading to the top, then took the footpath across the hill to a flight of stairs leading to the cell-house entrance. As he mounted the stairs, he realized he was in an exposed position, so he crouched and picked up his pace. About ten steps from the top of the stairs, he heard a gunshot from the cell house above him. A bullet ricocheted off the steps behind him. He dove into the ice plant growing along the stairway and scurried back down the hill, retracing his steps all the way to the bottom.

At the bottom of the hill, he met officer Ray Gaynor, who was making the rounds of the civilian dwellings to make sure the dependents were all locked inside. They talked quietly for a minute or two, then realized they were being called from above. "Hey, Oldham!"

Looking up, they saw Associate Warden Miller leaning over the rail of the lighthouse. "Somebody just got shot up here," he said. "Go around the hill and up the stairs and give whoever it is a hand. An officer was on the stairs and got shot by somebody inside the cell house."

"That was me up there, Mr. Miller!" Oldham shouted. "They missed me, and I ran back down here!"

"Well, go back up and check out the area and be sure there's nobody hurt up there. Then report back to me," Miller insisted.

Turning to Gaynor and shrugging his shoulders, Oldham smiled. "I wonder if Jughead expects me to find myself up there in that ice plant. I wonder if it has occurred to him that the son of a bitch that shot at me before might still be there and shoot at me again. He must really be shook up. What's going on, Ray?"

"I don't know, Hersh. All I know is the cons are

loose in the cell house and they've got guns. Pretty scary, huh?"

"Yeah, "I'm glad I'm out here and not on duty in there."

Oldham ran a short way up the hill, just to a point where he could see the area where he had been shot at. He stayed out of sight of the cell-house windows and confirmed what he already knew: he had been the only person shot at there. After carrying out his fruitless mission, he raced back down to the dock and complained again to Rychner that Associate Warden Miller had put him in jeopardy for nothing. The even-tempered Rychner tried to calm Oldham.

"Miller's under a lot of stress. They all are. We've got a lot more to worry about now than a few questionable orders, Hersh. Everything's okay down here, so why don't you ride up with the evening watch crew and get an assignment up top. They just arrived and are in the bus over there. You can report to the associate warden at that time, too. Chances are he'll want to make it right with you. He's not stupid, just scared."

"You're probably right, Rych," Oldham agreed. "It's just that Miller's normally such a solid guy that you get to the point where you don't expect him to ever make a stupid mistake." Shrugging the whole thing off, Oldham walked briskly to the waiting bus and headed toward the administration building.

Associate Warden Miller, though, was busy briefing the warden. He's just too old for the job, Miller thought after he finished briefing the seventy-two-year-old warden.

In 1912, the California governor chose James Johnston as warden of California's troubled maximum-security prison at Folsom. The prison was violent and chaotic, and the governor was under considerable pressure to clean it up. Although he had no prior penal experience, Johnston brought the situation under control within two years. He instituted antiviolence custodial procedures, improved living conditions for the inmates, and turned the former "hell hole" into a rehabilitation facility.

Thoroughly impressed by Johnston's success at Folsom, the governor appointed him warden of the huge prison at San Quentin. During his eleven-year tenure there, Johnston instituted many of the same changes he had made at Folsom, as well as others. He expanded the prison industries, developed an inmate road-building program, and recruited business and community leaders to assist in prisoner rehabilitation and job placement.

Johnston's progressive policies proved enormously successful. Recidivism fell off markedly. Over the years, hundreds of released inmates wrote letters of thanks to the warden for assisting them in straightening out their lives through education, work training, and attitudes learned while in prison. The California prison system became a model for the nation. Penology experts from around the world studied it. Johnston, more than anyone else, was responsible for the modern California prison system.

In 1933 Johnston was the California State Director of Penology. He was contacted by U.S. Attorney General Homer Cummings with the request that he become the warden of the new federal maximum-security prison to be established on Alcatraz the following year. Without hesitation, Johnston accepted. One of the nation's most liberal penologists became the head of the nation's toughest prison. In January 1934, Warden Johnston took charge of the island and in April of that year moved into his new home, only a few yards from the entrance to the cell house.

But he was no longer the vigorous, enlightened penology expert that Associate Warden Miller had met twelve years earlier, and it made Miller sad. It had been a gradual process, starting with the severe beating Johnston suffered at the hands of a crazed inmate a few years earlier. Disgruntled at what he considered unfair treatment, inmate Burton "Whitey" Phillips attacked the warden one day in the dining hall and inflicted serious head wounds that caused Johnston to be hospitalized for several days. Miller was concerned that despite the detailed briefing he had just given him, the warden did not have a good grasp of the situation. Johnston seemed hesitant and reluctant to take an aggressive approach to the situation. Armory Officer Fish had complained to Miller earlier about Johnston's inaction: "Hell, Ed, I couldn't even get him to make a decision about sounding the alarm."

"We have a very serious situation here, Mr. Miller," Johnston told the associate warden during the briefing. "I think it imperative that we call a meeting of all the senior supervisory personnel and outline a plan of action. But before we do anything, I think we must report the details to the Bureau [of Prisons] and then to the press. There will be many questions, and I believe the public deserves to know the status of things. I am particularly concerned about the presence of a machine gun in the cell house. I'm going to my office now to draft a telegram and make some calls. I'll be back here in ten or fifteen minutes. I'd like to have all the senior personnel presently on the island here at that time."

As the warden turned to leave, Miller interrupted him. "Yes, Sir, Warden, I'll get the lieutenants right up here. But keep in mind, Sir, the prisoners don't have a machine gun in there. The most they have is the rifle and pistol out of the gun gallery. The tommy guns are only in the towers, not in the gun galleries. There's no evidence of a tommy gun in the cell house."

"No, Mr. Miller, you're wrong," the old man shot back as he turned and walked into his office, shutting the door behind him.

Shaking his head, Miller walked to the armory and directed Fish to locate all the lieutenants on the island and summon them to his office right away. He then inquired as to whether the east gun gallery had been manned and, if so, by whom.

"Yeah, Ed," said Faulk, now acting as captain. "I sent Cochenour and Mullen to man the lower tier. Zubke and Long are in the upper level."

"I'm a little concerned about the Old Man, Ike,"

Miller said. "He's somehow got himself convinced that the cons are loose in there with a machine gun. That's just not so. If they had a tommy gun, Coy would have cut me in half. I'm afraid he's going to report that to the press and scare the living shit out of people. How are we doing on getting the work crews rounded up?"

"That ought to be pretty well underway," Faulk said.

Later, as the two men sat in the associate warden's office, Warden Johnston bustled in with a draft of his telegram to the press and the Bureau of Prisons. He handed Miller the handwritten dispatch and announced, "This is the message I want to go immediately."

Serious trouble. Convict has machine gun in the cell house. Have issued a riot call and placed armed guards at strategic locations. Most of our officers are imprisoned in the cell house. I cannot tell the extent of injuries suffered by our officers or the amount of damage done. Will give you more information later in the day when we get control.

James A. Johnston, Warden

Miller was aghast. He handed the message back to Johnston. "You really shouldn't send this, Warden. First of all, there's no evidence of a machine gun in the cell house. Secondly, it's not true that most of our officers are imprisoned there."

Annoyed at Miller's resistance, Johnston gestured

at the message angrily. "Have this sent to all the newspapers and radio stations in the area. I'll be in my office. When the lieutenants are here, I want to see you all in my office." He turned and walked away.

"Jesus Christ!" Miller said. "I don't know what's gotten into him. This is going to cause one hell of a stir in town. At most, there's ten guys in there. The cons have no more than the two guns from the gallery. He's out of touch with reality."

Ike Faulk sighed. "Yeah, but Ed, he's the boss. We just work here."

Miller handed the paper to Mills and directed him to send it to the four San Francisco papers, the Oakland papers, the wire services, and the six major Bay Area radio stations.

In the lower tier of the east gun gallery, Virgil Cochenour and John Mullen crouched behind the protective steel shield. At the north end Cochenour surveyed the area between A Block and B Block, looking for any sign of movement. At the other end Mullen peered over the steel plate, studying Seedy Street and C Block. Both men had views directly down Broadway as they cautiously moved back and forth along the gallery.

After little more than half an hour at his post, Mullen saw a tall convict moving between C Block and D Block and got off a quick blast of his shotgun. He missed, and the inmate ducked safely into the officers' toilet at the west end of C Block. He guessed it was Coy, the only prisoner who had been identified by Miller. A short time later, Mullen observed a short inmate wearing an officer's uniform jacket come around the end of C Block. He fired and missed again, and the short man ducked back behind the cell block.

It was now obvious to the three remaining convicts that their movements would be dramatically curtailed. "There's screws in the east gallery," Cretzer warned Hubbard as the two stood behind C Block. "They just took shots at me and Coy."

17

At 3:45 the final bell rang at San Francisco's Marina Junior High. Fifteen hundred young people flooded onto Bay, Chestnut, and Fillmore Streets. The sun controlled the sky, holding the afternoon fog bank out at sea, well to the west of the Golden Gate. A fresh breeze pushed a few sailboats around the bay and cooled the sunbathers on Marina Green.

Soon, though, the fog would ease through the Golden Gate, spill over the Marin hills, and blot out the sky until next midmorning. It would enter the Bay as a thin gray finger pointed directly at Alcatraz Island. The fog would shroud the island, leaving it in premature twilight while the sun still bathed the rest of the bay. As the fog shrouded Alcatraz, the booming foghorns on the western shore of the island would begin singing their two-note lament, a sound as familiar to everyone in the Bay Area as the squawking of the seagulls. With the fog would come the piercing wind, which always made it seem colder than it actually was.

It was still sunny, however, as thirteen-year-old Ernie Lageson Jr. pushed his way onto a crowded streetcar and presented his student ticket to the conductor. There were more than a hundred copies of the *San Francisco Call-Bulletin* waiting for him at the corner of Van Ness and Clay Streets. Ernie sat impatiently. All the newspapers had to be delivered before 5:30, and today was collection day.

As he tossed his newspaper bag on the sidewalk next to the papers, he glanced at the late-news box in the lower left-hand corner of the front page. It was always printed in red ink. This portion of the paper carried the latest news bulletins, inserted moments before the edition went to press. Ernie felt his heart come into his mouth as he read the lead bulletin: *ALCATRAZ BREAK—Prisoners Have Machine Gun in Cell-house.* The narrative that followed was frustratingly brief: *Convicts control prison armory. Riot call issued.*

Young Ernie tried to assure himself that his dad would be okay. After all, this was not the first time he'd heard of escape attempts—attempts that were ultimately unsuccessful. Nor was it the first time he had learned of an escape attempt from a newspaper headline. He had read headlines describing an escape attempt in August 1943 as he and two of his friends returned to the island following a summer Saturday in the city. It had frightened him then, too, even though he knew the island to be virtually escape-proof. That time, the escape attempt had turned out to be just a convict's walking away from the prison laundry. He made his way to the rocky beach but was quickly captured. Ernie had also been on the island in April 1943, when a group of escapees made it into the water. He recalled the deafening sound of the escape siren and the distant sound of gunfire as a tower guard shot and killed one of the escapees.

But there was something in this news report Ernie had never heard before: *Prisoners Have Machine Gun in Cell-house. Convicts control prison armory.* That seemed an impossibility. If it was true, it was the most frightening thing that could happen on Alcatraz.

He read and reread the bulletin. He thought the paper must have it wrong. The editors must have been making up a story because they didn't know what was really going on.

The more he thought about it, the more convinced Ernie was that the report had to be wrong. There was no way that prisoners could capture the armory. His father had explained to him that the armory could only be entered through electrically controlled doors and gates operated by the armory officer located inside the tiny bastille. The armory officer had to see, identify, and pass through anyone who entered. In addition, the standing order from the warden was that no door or gate was to be opened to permit or further an escape, even if the prisoners held hostages.

Ernie decided it was equally unlikely that the

prisoners could have a machine gun, or any other kind of gun. Officers like his father who were in contact with the inmates carried no firearms. Only the guards in the towers and gun galleries were armed. The gun galleries were accessible only from outside the cell house. Machine guns were issued only to the tower guards, all of whom were outside and at considerable distances from the cell house. The report had to be wrong.

Still, Ernie had a nagging doubt. Prisoners Have Machine Gun. He had never seen that kind of mistake before. Convicts with a machine gun would be horrible, he thought. Those guys would kill everyone in sight. No, it could never happen.

Ernie's thoughts turned to his friends who lived on the island, all of whom were out of mainland schools by now and at the dock waiting for the boat home. It would be an exciting time at Pier Four because, like Ernie, they would know that the newspaper story couldn't be right. But how could the paper possibly make such an error? Could there be some basis for it? Anxious to get home and hear the latest news on the radio, Ernie quickly filled his bag with newspapers and hurriedly completed his route.

18

At 4:00 the warden sat down to review the situation with Associate Warden Miller and Lieutenants Boatman, Faulk, and Roberts. The industry and outside workforce was back in the recreation yard. Extra guards were stationed on the yard wall. Wary of possible gunfire from inside the cell house, they were standing their watch inside the blockhouses at the corners of the wall. Lieutenant Rychner, in charge of the dock, had ordered the prison launch to circle the island and remain in constant radio contact with the armory. Fish sent word to those meeting in the warden's office that Officer Besk in the Hill Tower had been wounded and needed to be relieved. Levinson and Comerford had been shot at but were unhurt. Ten officers in the cell house were unaccounted for. Miller said that he had sent armed details to maintain surveillance of all cell-house exits. The status of Stucker in the basement and the possible involvement of his men was unknown. The hospital reported everything normal. It was again pointed out to the warden that, in the opinion of Miller and all the lieutenants, the inmates did not have a machine gun, but at most had a rifle, a pistol, and a total of seventy-one rounds of ammunition.

Everyone was concerned that there were as many as 135 inmates in the cell house who could participate in the uprising, although senior officers all believed that a mass breakout was no longer possible. They were also concerned with the status of the ten missing officers.

Associate Warden Miller was especially concerned about the officers' safety. "We've just got to get some men in there to rescue those guys. What if it were us in there? Wouldn't we want somebody to come get us?" He pointed out that every minute of delay was dangerous. Miller continued to urge that a detail of volunteers be assembled to storm the cell house.

Warden Johnston would have none of it. "Mr. Miller, it has been a long-standing policy at this penitentiary that firearms are not permitted on the floor of the cell house. I do not intend to modify that policy now. The introduction of further firearms into the cell house under the present conditions could, in my opinion, lead to catastrophic results, and I will not sanction it. In addition, I do not feel that we are at sufficient custodial strength to attempt any armed intervention at this time. I also do not think we should consider any type of attack on the cell house until we have better information as to the location of the insurgents. Given the fact that Mr. Oldham was shot at from C or D Block, we can't be sure where they are."

It was obvious by the looks on their faces that the lieutenants were not happy with Johnston's assessment of the situation. All of them shared Miller's view that an armed assault on the cell house should be carried out as soon as possible. The rioters had shot at three of the towers, so there was a real fear that some of the hostages had also been shot and might need immediate medical attention.

"I have requested support from the U.S. Marine Corps," Johnston said. "And I have been advised that within an hour or two a battle group will be dispatched. I believe these men should relieve our officers on the wall and other sentry posts, freeing up custodial personnel to enter the cell house. I think we are doing everything we can at this time. I have notified the Coast Guard, the Army, the Navy, the San Francisco Police Department, and the Bureau of Prisons. I have requested medical support and air cover. Additionally, I have called Warden Duffy at San Quentin for reinforcements and have also requested help from the wardens at McNeil Island, Leavenworth, and Atlanta. Keep me advised as our off-duty officers return during the next few hours. Keep me informed of all developments. I think we're doing everything we can, and that'll be it for now." With that, Johnston dismissed the officers.

Miller fumed as he left the warden's office. "I

can't believe we're not going in there," he complained to Faulk. "What the hell do we need with the
Army, Navy, and Marine Corps? And air cover? Our
people can handle this thing. The cons have only got
two guns and the ammo they got from the gun
gallery. We've got to go in there and get our guys
out. I'm sending an assault team into the west gallery, no matter what he says."

The lieutenants were in total agreement. They
were all hardened custodial veterans and knew the
danger of inaction. Each would have immediately
volunteered to follow Miller into the cell house to
rescue their fellow officers. Miller selected Officers
Herald Gallagher, Joseph Maxwell, and Harold Stites.
He directed them to draw weapons and attempt to
man the west gun gallery.

After receiving their weapons, the three men
made their way cautiously around the southeast corner of the cell house and along the catwalk on the
south side. Reaching the door to the gallery, Maxwell
opened the outer barred door and peered through
the small bulletproof glass window in the inner, solid
steel door. Inside he saw Coy, wearing an officer's
uniform and carrying a rifle, standing twenty feet
away. He saw no officers but noted that the door
between D Block and the cell house was wide open.

Maxwell aimed his machine gun at the window
and attempted to shoot it out. Despite using up
nearly an entire clip of ammunition, he succeeded in
only shattering the bulletproof glass and calling
Coy's attention to his presence outside the door. Coy
reacted instantly. He dove toward the open cell-

house door and fired a single shot through the steel door, missing Maxwell by inches. All three guards dropped to the deck. Grimacing with impotence, stunned by their failure, the three decided not to attempt to enter the gallery but to report the events to Miller and await further instructions.

Miller agreed with their decision not to try another entry at that time. He then stationed several officers on the hill below the cell house to set up a barrage of gunfire into D Block.

A shadow again appeared on the floor in front of Ernie Lageson and the other conscious officers in cell 403. The three held their breath and remained motionless. This time it was Hubbard with the butcher knife. He studied the bodies in the two cells, looking for any change in their positions. He stood for a moment in front of cell 403, then moved to cell 402, where he looked for several seconds at the motionless Baker and Simpson. Back at cell 403, he stood for a few moments before sticking the knife back into his waistband. Satisfied that all the men in the cells were dead, he walked quickly back to the west end and to the cell-house desk.

When he was gone, Lageson and Burdett moved slightly to ease their aching legs and backs from their cramped positions, stretching their arms and legs.

"How's Weinhold look, Joe?" Lageson asked.

"He's breathing, but he's hit real bad," Burdett said. "He was moaning just a moment ago before Hubbard got here, but thank God, he stopped."

The eerie, unnatural quiet of the cell house was shattered by the sound of gunfire. Shotgun pellets ricocheted off the floor in front of the hostage cells, followed by the muffled voices of the convicts somewhere at the west end of the cell house. The three conscious guards in cell 403 were elated.

"Those shots came from the east gallery," Burdett whispered.

"Yeah," Bristow said from under the bunk. "It sounds like something's beginning to happen out there. Maybe they're going to be able to get us out of here pretty soon."

"I hope so, cause I really gotta take a leak," Burdett said.

"You know, Joe, if I wasn't so goddam scared I could probably think of something funny to say right now," Lageson said. But nobody laughed.

"If they've got guys in the east gallery who can fire down Seedy Street, that may keep Coy and the rest of those assholes at the west end and away from these cells," Lageson said.

After only a few minutes, another shotgun blast from the east gallery sprayed buckshot down the corridor. The whispering voices of the convicts sounded more excited than before. None of them, however, appeared in front of the cells.

Lageson checked his watch, carefully moving his sleeve. It was after five. They had been in the cell for more than three hours. Weinhold began to stir and moan. He mumbled deliriously about his daughter's birthday party, then made some unintelligible reference to water. They listened sympathetically to the badly wounded man, fearing that his groaning would alert the convicts.

"Let's try giving him some water, Ernie," Burdett said. "Put some water in my hand, and I'll drip it into his mouth. Maybe that'll help."

Lageson cautiously turned on the sink faucet, permitting a small amount of water to drip into his cupped hand but making little sound. He poured the water into Burdett's hand. Burdett dripped about a teaspoon of the liquid into the captain's mouth. This process was repeated several times until Weinhold, apparently comfortable, fell silent. Once again the cell house was eerily quiet. The only sounds the hostages could hear were the muted voices of the three desperate men at the end of the cell block.

Once again the silence was shattered, this time by the explosive blast of a machine gun. Two lengthy bursts from the tommy gun were followed by a single rifle shot. Shouting and yelling erupted in D Block.

"Nice shooting, Bernie. You nailed him." It was the voice of Joe Cretzer.

"Yeah, I'm sure I got him!" Coy exclaimed.

The hostages in cell 403 listened intently, but no one spoke.

19

The warden was furious. "Mr. Miller, you should not have ordered that assault. We do not have sufficient manpower at this time to attempt any assaults on the cell house. One of those men was almost killed. Safety must be given the highest priority. The Marines have promised a detachment, which should be arriving soon. Once they are on the scene, they can relieve our men on the wall and we can then reassess our personnel strength. The Coast Guard has also agreed to pick up the off-duty officers and bring them to the island. Within the next couple of hours, we'll be in a position to determine our next step. I'll be in my office if you need me."

Safety, hell! Miller thought, fuming inwardly at Johnston's position. We've got to get in there and get our guys out! This waiting for the Marines and all our off-duty personnel is for the birds. We can't wait another couple of hours to decide what we're gonna do.

But the associate warden's hands were tied. There was nothing he could do but wait and maintain control of things. He ordered more men to be stationed on the hill below the cell house, where the barrage into D Block continued. All the outside inmates were safely in the yard. All possible exits from the cell house were under armed surveillance. There was no possibility of a mass breakout.

Shortly after five-thirty, Johnston delivered a message to his secretary, Walter Bertrand, for dispatch to the press:

> *Have no additional information any more accurate or detailed than I have already given you. Our situation is difficult and precarious. Our officers are all being used in every place we can man. The armed prisoner or prisoners are still eluding us so that at the moment we cannot control them. The Navy, Coast Guard and San Francisco Police Dept. are standing by to help when we find we can use them to advantage.*
>
> *James A. Johnston, Warden*

While the guards poured gunfire into the cell house and thousands of spectators jammed the hills, bridges and waterfronts of the city, the Matson liner Monterey plowed smoothly through San Francisco Bay. As the pilot eased the huge luxury liner down the center of the channel, the Hawaii-bound vessel passed a scant 400 yards from the southwest tip of the island. The passengers, most still in the midst of their bon-voyage parties and wearing flower leis and brightly colored aloha shirts, crowded the rails on the starboard side as the ship passed the island. As many of the passengers and crew focused binoculars on the cell house and the hill below to observe the gunfire, others cheered, threw confetti, and waived miniature flags. The drama unfolding on Alcatraz was added excitement to an already exciting cruise to the magic Hawaiian Islands.

Just before 6:00 that evening, Ernie Jr. returned home and found the small apartment empty. But with trouble in the cell house, his father would have missed the 5:00 boat and might even miss the 5:40. That would delay his return until after 7:00. Ernie tried to think positively, but his mind kept returning to the story that the prisoners had guns, even a machine gun. Nothing had ever upset him like this. He knew his dad was the cell-house officer. He had to be in jeopardy. What if he had died?

Ernie turned on the radio and switched from one station to another. All the reports were fragmentary and incomplete, typical of all Alcatraz news coverage. But every news report he heard echoed the same sickening facts: the rioting prisoners controlled the cell house and they had guns. The bulletin in the newspaper must have been correct. As hard as it was to believe, it must be true. Ernie knew that in all the escape attempts in the island's history there had never been an instance when an inmate had a gun. The prisoners must have gotten into a gun gallery, he thought. Maybe a tower, even, but surely not the armory. But it didn't matter where they got them. An inmate with a gun was trouble, desperate trouble.

The radio reports became more frequent. The networks had all set up remote broadcast sites along the waterfront and atop the hills overlooking the island. They were broadcasting continuous accounts of the jailbreak and even had occasional bulletins from boats off-shore. There was a report that a call had gone out to the Coast Guard and that two Coast Guard cutters were now stationed near the island. A San Francisco police boat was patrolling the area, they said. From boats near the island, reporters were describing the gunfire coming from outside the cell house into the windows of the building. Explosions and tracer bullets could be seen on the south and west sides of the island as prison personnel fired into the cell-house windows. The situation was well beyond anything Ernie had ever heard before at Alcatraz.

On the bay, dozens of boats lay just outside the permanent buoys that marked the 200 restricted zone. Most of the boats were privately owned and filled with sightseers. Using binoculars, they gazed up at the forbidding prison building and watched the pyrotechnic display as the tracer bullets flashed into the cell-house windows. Now five Coast Guard boats, two Navy ships, and the San Francisco Police

Department launch lay just off the island. Star shells fired by the Navy ships provided a surreal effect. As they exploded 2,500 feet in the air, the blue-white light descended by parachute, illuminating the entire island for a minute or so before burning out and falling into the water. Overhead a Navy PBY aircraft circled the island at a very low altitude. The prison launch also continued to circle the island.

By this time, the hilltops throughout the city were jammed with observers. From vantage points atop Telegraph and Russian Hills, the Presidio, the Marina, and the North Beach waterfronts, thousands of San Franciscans crowded together to watch the gun battle. Police struggled to cope with traffic jams as hundreds of motorists tried to find somewhere to park and watch the extraordinary event. Hundreds of people jammed the rails of the Golden Gate Bridge, observing the activities along the west and south sides of the island with binoculars.

Finally, Ernie found one station quoting the telegram sent by Alcatraz Warden James Johnston to the press. There was no longer any doubt. The convicts were armed, and a violent outbreak was underway. The cell house was under the control of the armed rioters. Ernie's father was very likely imprisoned inside. Ernie couldn't shrug off the grim news stories as exaggerations any longer. His father was almost certainly a hostage.

Much later than usual, Ernie's mother hurried to the bus stop at Sacramento and Sansome Streets.

Eunice Lageson had stayed late at work listening to news reports on one of the radios in the office, then she had scanned the late editions of the afternoon papers for news of the riot. There was not much detail being reported, but there was news. Horrible news. Convicts loose in the cell house with a machine gun. It was unthinkable. She was sick with worry. She thought of her family as she quickened her pace. Ernie Sr., the cell-house officer, was undoubtedly a hostage if he were still alive. And Ernie Jr. was home alone.

The bus ride home seemed to last forever. When Eunice arrived at the apartment, Ernie Jr. was at the door to greet her. They threw their arms around one another.

"Do you think Dad's okay?"

"I don't know, Son. We'll just have to wait and pray to God that everything will be all right."

Eunice again tried to contact the island by phone, but she wasn't surprised to get a busy signal. She had been trying all afternoon from work. There were only two private lines from the mainland to the island, and the phone was in the armory. There was a pay phone in the administrative offices, but neither Ernie nor his mother knew that number. Eunice had called the armory repeatedly without success.

Darkness fell. "Why hasn't Dad or somebody called?" Ernie asked repeatedly, but his mother had no answer. Lageson's job as main cell-house officer put him at the very heart of the prison population. The report from the warden had said that most of the prison's officers were imprisoned in the cell house. Ernie knew his father had to be in there somewhere—wounded, taken hostage, perhaps dead.

At last Eunice got through and could hear the phone at the other end of the line ringing. "I got through," she cried out, "it's ringing!"

Armory Officer Cliff Fish answered and sounded surprisingly calm. "Eunice, I guess you know we're having a little trouble out here, but we should have things straightened out real soon."

"Have you seen Ernie? Is he okay?"

"Well, he was around here this afternoon, but I haven't seen him lately. I'll pass your message along to him. I really have to hang up. We need this line to be kept open."

Eunice hung up in resigned distress. Her son read the despair in her eyes. "He's not coming home, is he, Mom? Is he dead?" Tears welled up in his eyes.

"I don't know, Honey, but they don't seem to know where he is. He's probably one of the men in the cell house. We'll just have to wait till they can get him out. In the meantime, let's pray for Dad and the other men in there with him."

Oh, God! Ernie thought. I'll never see my dad again. We'll never again sunbathe or Indian-wrestle on the lawns in Lafayette Park, or swim at Fleischacker Pool, or go to another Seals game. Images flashed of all the wonderful things they had done together, particularly on his father's days off during the summer, when there were just the two of them. There were so many fun times and good talks. He prayed desperately to have his dad back again.

"Please, God. Let him come home."

Eunice sat stoically at the kitchen table listening to the news broadcasts. She imagined what her life would be like without her companion of fifteen years. They had been through so much together. For ten years they had struggled during the brutal economic times of the Great Depression while Ernie labored as a teacher in North Dakota. Then, just when things had gotten better with the move to California, Ernie left for World War II. The stint at Alcatraz after the war was intended to be temporary. After graduate studies in the summer, Ernie had planned to return to teaching. Oh, if only he had left the prison sooner, Eunice thought.

"How about a couple of games of cribbage, Honey?" she suggested. "It might help make the time go faster."

"Okay, Mom," Ernie replied, trying to be cheerful. He set up the board and cards at the kitchen table.

At about 6:00 that evening, an assault boat carrying a Marine combat team in full battle dress had tied up at the Alcatraz dock. They were ushered to the main cell house, where they took positions on the yard wall. The Marines were to stand guard over the approximately 140 prisoners who were out of the cell house when the riot began and were now confined in the recreation yard.

When the Marines were stationed on the wall, some of the inmates called out, taunting the new arrivals. "Hey, look! We've got some soldier boys up there on the wall. I'm really scared. Fuck you, Jar Heads."

The battle-hardened veterans of Tarawa, Iwo Jima, and Okinawa weren't as easygoing as the prison guards. The young troops whipped off the safeties of their M-1 rifles and aimed them directly into the groups of prisoners below. The convicts suddenly had second thoughts about provoking the Marines.

"I hope one of those bastards down there tries something," a baby-faced corporal said to his buddy. "I'd love to blow the head off one of those worthless motherfuckers."

The presence of the Marines seemed to improve Warden Johnston's spirits. With the available man-power nearly doubled, he now spoke with more confidence and seemed less nervous. But Associate Warden Miller found it increasingly difficult to communicate with Johnston, who from the outset of the crisis had alternated his time between his office and his toilet.

"Okay, Warden, the Marines are here. We need to get those hostages out of there," he said.

"Not now, Mr. Miller," the warden said. "We need more information. Where are the insurgents? You don't know. Where are you going to attack? You'd just be setting yourself up."

"But the men who are now in the east gun gallery say there's no prisoner activity in the cell house. Only in D Block and the western end of the cell house around C Block. It is not a mass riot or breakout, Warden. It's just a few prisoners with two guns, a rifle and a pistol, and a handful of bullets, most of which they've already used."

"Not yet, Mr. Miller." The warden turned and walked into his office.

Outside, the spring daylight had faded. The lighting inside the cell house was dim. It was difficult to see. The shooting from outside into D Block continued. In cells 402 and 403 the drama continued. Weinhold was in a state of delirium, and the others couldn't keep him quiet. He cried about not being able to go to his daughter's birthday party, while Ernie Lageson and the others cringed, expecting that his cries would be heard by the inmates. The guards knew that Coy and Cretzer must have already used most of the ammunition they captured from Burch. So Hubbard's knife they would feel if the rioters learned that any of the hostages were still alive. The three conscious officers had to keep Weinhold quiet.

"Let's try giving him some more water," Lageson whispered.

"Okay, Ernie, it's about all we can do," Burdett agreed, still uncomfortably sprawled across the end of the bunk. Again the trickle of water quieted the unconscious man.

By now Ernie Lageson was in considerable pain from both his facial wound and cramped position. He had been forced to maintain the crumpled pose now for several hours. Burdett, too, was in pain due to his awkward pose. Cecil Corwin was grossly disfigured by his wound. He sat stoically, propped against the wall. The only sound he made was an occasional bubbling as he tried to clear the blood from his breathing passages. In the adjoining cell, both Simpson and Baker were unconscious but fortunately made no sound. Among the hostages Burdett, Bristow, and Sundstrom were unhurt. Sundstrom lay motionless and silent under the bunk.

As the shells crashed into D Block, Lageson noticed Coy, Cretzer, and Hubbard were moving in and out of the C Block utility corridor. It appeared that the inmates were settling into the utility corridor for their last stand. Since the east gun gallery was now manned, the escapees weren't making inspections of the hostage cell as frequently. "Thank God," Lageson muttered.

Associate Warden Miller had just returned from supervising the gun crews on the hill below the cell house and was excited when he was told to report to the warden's office. Hundreds of rounds were being pumped into D Block, but due to the angle of fire, most of them were ineffective. The bars on the windows deflected much of the gunfire, and most of the gas grenades bounced off the bars, falling harmlessly to the ground below. A few had started small grass fires, which quickly burned themselves out. Ineffective as this assault was, it was all the associate warden could do and remain within his orders. To the outside world watching from ship and shore, it looked like a mighty armed struggle in progress.

"Mr. Miller," the warden said, "I want you to order Lieutenant Bergen and Officer Cochrane to visualize the interior of the west end of the cell house. They can place a ladder against the outside wall of the cell house and look in the windows."

"But Warden," Miller interrupted, "we know from the reports out of the east gun gallery that there is no activity in the cell house. All the prisoners are out of sight. For two men to try to look in the windows will accomplish little more than to silhouette them against the outside light and expose them to possible convict gunfire."

"You have your orders, Mr. Miller." Once again the warden retreated into his office and closed the door.

Miller located Bergen and Cochrane and advised them of the warden's request. Both men immediately agreed to carry out the mission but raised the same questions that Miller had.

"Sure Ed, we'll climb up there," Bergen said. "But what the hell does the Old Man think we're gonna see? It'll be dark in the cell house, and I doubt that we'll be able to see a damn thing. I'll be a 'sitting duck' out there on a ladder in front of the window."

"Hey, Phil, I've already told him that," Miller said. "But this is what he wants done and, you know as well as I do, that when he makes up his mind there's no way to change it. If you guys don't want to go, just say so, and I'll see..."

"Don't get me wrong, Ed," Bergen interrupted. "Of course, we'll go. Hell, why can't we just knock off all this bullshit and go into the cell house for the hostages?"

The two men drew their weapons and made their way to the northwest corner of the cell house. They pulled an extension ladder off the fire truck and propped it against the outside wall under one of the windows. With Cochrane at ground level to steady the ladder, Bergen climbed slowly to the top and peered into the barred window, approximately thirty feet above the ground. As they expected, it was dark inside.

"What do you see?" Cochrane called out.

"Not a goddam thing," Bergen said. "And I'm coming down. This is a waste of time. At least I didn't get shot."

20

B ernie Coy slipped into cell 404, the cell used as
the guards' toilet. While he was seated on the
commode, he saw the fading light glitter off
something on the floor under the bunk. Reaching
down under the bunk, Coy grasped a key. Holding
it up to the light, he read the number, 107. "Son of
a bitch! Now that it's too fucking late!" He slipped
the key into his pocket.

Back at the west end of the cell house, Coy
slipped the key into the lock. He didn't really know
what he would do if the door opened. But the lock
had been so abused by the use of improper keys
that even key 107 wouldn't open the door. Shrugging his shoulders, Coy slipped the key back into his
pocket.

It had been more than twenty minutes since any

of the prisoners had checked on the hostages. Reassured by the fact that the gunfire seemed to be occupying the escapees' attention, Ernie Lageson rose to his feet and stretched his aching back and leg muscles. It had been hours since he had been shot. His entire body was tired and aching. Burdett had finally given in and had shifted his body closer to the center of the bunk before helplessly urinating on himself and the bed clothing.

Rummaging through his pockets, Ernie Lageson found a pencil. On the wall he wrote the names of the six prisoners involved in the attempted break. Cretzer. Coy. Carnes. Hubbard. Thompson. Shockley. He circled the names of Cretzer, Coy, and Hubbard and placed a check after Cretzer's name. Even if we don't get out of here, at least there'll be some record of who was involved in this thing, he thought.

He looked around the cell at the three wounded men, all unconscious or silently enduring their wounds. Although his own wound was still painful, he said a silent prayer of thanks that he had so far survived.

At 7:00 Miller was finally able to convince the warden to authorize another assault on the west gun gallery. He promised Warden Johnston that no guns would be taken into the cell house. He reminded Johnston that entry into the gun gallery was from outside the prison. Since none of the prisoners were in the gun gallery, there was no way any more guns could fall into convict hands.

Miller next assembled a group of senior officers, including Bergen. Miller himself led the team along the catwalk on the south side of the cell house to the outside gallery door. At the entry, Bergen prevailed upon Miller to let him lead the squad into the gallery. "Ed, you'd better not go in there and run the risk of getting shot. We really need you out there in the front office running things. With both you and Weinhold out of commission, God knows what Johnston might do. Let me and a couple of other guys go in there. You stay here. We'll report back to you." Miller reluctantly agreed.

Bergen drew his pistol, Stites carried a machine gun, and Cochrane also had a pistol. The three men threw open the doors to the gallery and rushed in facing a barrage of inmate gunfire. With weapons blazing, Bergen and Cochrane turned right to climb the ladder to the second level. Stites headed to the left and stood with his back against the wall, firing repeated bursts from his machine gun into D Block. As Cochrane reached the ladder, he took a bullet in his left shoulder. It spun him around, and he fell in a crumpled heap on the floor. Bergen stepped over his friend and scrambled up the ladder. Stites followed closely behind. But Cochrane was just hit, not dead. Still firing his pistol with his right hand, his left arm hanging limp at his his side, Cochrane got to his feet and backed out the door to the safety of the catwalk. He was able to make it back to the emergency medical station in the administrative offices without assistance.

The area now became a war zone. At the gallery

entrance, two guards at a time stepped into the doorway and sprayed machine-gun fire into D Block. When their guns were empty, they were replaced by two more gunners. The withering barrage went on unabated as more officers slipped into the gallery and mounted the ladder to the second level. As they sprayed bullets into the gallery, many bullets hit the bars and steel screens of the gallery and ricocheted around the cell block. Amazingly, from the hill below, some officers continued to fire rifles into D Block, unaware that the moving figures inside D Block were their fellow officers. From inside the gallery, the guards fired blindly into D Block and at the cell-house door. Cretzer in D Block and Coy in the cell-house doorway returned the fire but were running out of ammunition. It was total chaos. Only the prisoners knew at whom they were shooting.

Once on the second level, Lieutenant Bergen began a search for Bert Burch, the gun-gallery officer. Crawling on his hands and knees, he entered the cell-house side of the gallery with his automatic pistol cocked and ready to fire. To his surprise he quickly came face to face with Burch, who was also on his hands and knees behind the steel shield. Shivering in his underwear and uniform shirt, Burch was stiff and sore but otherwise unhurt.

"Bert!" exclaimed the astonished Bergen. "Are you okay?"

"Yeah," Burch said, smiling, happy to finally be rescued. "Yeah, I'm okay, but I'm freezing my ass off up here. The fuckers took my pants." Burch described Coy's attack and how he was subsequently able to free himself. He knew that Coy, Cretzer, and Hubbard were involved but didn't know anything about the other participants or the hostages.

When he reached the second level of the gallery, Stites dropped to his hands and knees. He crawled down the south extension of the gallery and peered over the steel shield into the D Block cells. He could see some of the inmates in their cells. He noticed that many had rigged protective barriers across the fronts of their cells.

Officers Oldham and Fred Mahan entered next, emptying their guns into D Block. Mahan scaled the ladder and joined Bergen as Oldham scrambled up behind him. Oldham had just reached the second level when a bullet tore into his right arm. The force of the impact spun him around and knocked him to the floor. He fell across the ladder-well and cried out in pain, "They got me! I'm hit!" As he lay there trying to steady himself, Oldham was aware of Stites stepping over him. Through the din of the gunfire, Oldham heard Stites calmly announce, "Boys, they got me, too." He collapsed on top of Oldham. Blood poured from a gaping wound in Stites's back. He slipped forward down the ladder. Oldham grabbed wildly for the falling body. He was able to clutch Stites's uniform jacket and prevent the injured man from falling headfirst to the level below.

Oldham's own wound made it impossible for him to move the mortally wounded Stites. He called for help. Finally, his cries were heard over the blast of gunfire. Officers from outside entered to remove Stites, who now appeared to be dying. Only a few years earlier, the courageous Stites had single-hand-edly stopped a prison break. Now he was the first fatality of the Battle at Alcatraz. As Stites's body was removed, Officer Fred Richberger took a bullet in the leg and had to be assisted to the first-aid station. The sight of wounded officers being carried from the gallery brought loud cheers from the inmates in the yard below.

"Hey look! They nailed a couple of the screws!" one of the cons yelled. More cheering followed.

Bergen and Burch moved over to the D Block side of the gallery. The wounded men were replaced by other officers, and the D Block side of the gallery was secured. Bergen then returned to the cell-house side and crawled to the north end of the gallery, periodically peeking over the protective steel shield. He neither saw nor heard anything in the cell blocks below. Except for the gunfire coming into D Block, there was no sound at all. At the north end of the gallery, he raced up the ladder to the top tier. It appeared empty, so he crawled slowly back to the D Block side, again periodically stopping to look over the shield down into the cell house. At the door he paused briefly, then returned to the D Block side. It was quiet except for the rifle fire coming into D Block from the hill below.

With the entire gallery secure, Bergen picked up the phone—one of the phones that had rung so impotently all afternoon—and reported to the armory. After making his status report and telling Fish that there was absolutely no inmate activity in either D Block or the cell house, he requested that some clothes be sent down for Burch. Bergen manned the upper tier. The others remained in the tier below throughout the night.

During the fusillade that accompanied the invasion of the gun gallery, Cretzer had darted out of the second-tier D Block cell in which he was hiding, down the stairs, and into the relative safety of the cell house. Coy had earlier retreated from D Block and had been firing at the invaders through the open cell-house door. Coy, Cretzer, and Hubbard heard the sounds of the guards moving around in the gallery. They realized that with both galleries manned, their movement within the cell house was severely limited. They knew that there would soon be continuous gunfire from the galleries and that they now likely faced the final hours of their lives. Checking their remaining ammunition and picking up gas masks, they took up positions in the C Block utility corridor. There they would be safe from gunfire yet able to climb to the top of the cell block and fire at the guards. Climbing up the wall inside the corridor, Coy and Cretzer surveyed the cell house from the top of C Block.

"How long you think we can hold out up here?" Cretzer asked Coy.

"Until we get them or they get us," Coy replied.

In the growing darkness, they heard gunshots fired into D Block from the west gallery and from outside the building. The gunfire was interspersed with shouted demands by Bergen that they throw out their guns and surrender.

"Those assholes think we're still over in D

Block," Cretzer said, smirking. "And as long as they do, we can probably nail a few screws from up here when they come through the main gate."

21

In their apartment on Sacramento Street, Eunice and Ernie Jr. continued their cribbage game. The 8:00 radio-news broadcast reported that two officers, Harry Cochrane and Fred Richberger, had been wounded in an apparent attempt to retake the cell house. Cochrane was badly injured, but neither man was gravely wounded. Both Ernie and his mother knew the officers. Word of their being shot made their fears for Ernie Sr. terrifyingly real. Eunice's first thoughts were of the wives of the wounded men. Ernie continued to worry that he would never again see his father alive. Maybe if I turn on the ball game, he thought, I'll think about something else.

For a little while his plan worked. He listened to the bottom of the Seal lineup as shortstop Roy Nicely, catcher Joe Sprinz, and pitcher Ray Harrell all went down quietly in their half of the third inning.

But between innings there were ghastly descriptions of flying bullets, exploding tear-gas bombs, and the desperate situation on Alcatraz. As Ernie lay in bed, listening to the radio and sick at heart, a reporter broadcasting from Pier Four described the arrival of the Alcatraz launch and dramatically announced that "one guard has now been positively identified as dead." The announcement took Ernie's breath. He was frozen with fright.

"The dead guard is Harold Stites," the reporter continued. "His body, along with several injured officers, has just been removed from the Alcatraz launch. The injured men are being taken immediately to Marine Hospital for treatment. They are all expected to survive." Ernie's heart pounded as he lunged off the bed and raced to his mother's side.

"Did you hear that, Mom? Mr. Stites has been killed, and a bunch of other guards have been shot."

The blood drained out of Eunice's face. She slumped in her chair. "My God!" she whispered. "The Stiteses have four kids."

Tears streamed down Ernie's cheeks. "Please, God," he prayed, this time out loud. "Please, bring Dad back."

22

Associate Warden Miller now pushed Warden Johnston to allow him to lead an assault team into the cell house to rescue the hostages. Warden Johnston had been encouraged by the recapture of the west gun gallery, but he still refused to permit an armed rescue attempt. Instead, he ordered that efforts be made to convince the inmates to surrender.

"Sir, I really believe that if they had any notion of surrendering, we'd have heard from them before now," Miller said. "There are telephones all over the cell house that they could use to call out and ask for a deal."

"I don't think we should do anything more of a violent nature until we've exhausted all possibilities of a peaceful conclusion," Johnston said. "I really think we should consider the possibility of their surrender. With both gun galleries occupied, maybe the inmates will view their situation differently."

"Okay, Sir, we'll give it a try," Miller said half-heartedly. Miller grabbed a megaphone and made his way around the southeast corner of the cell house to one of the broken D Block windows. As he walked alone along the catwalk, he signaled to the rifle teams below. "Hold your fire! Hold your fire!"

Turning the megaphone to the window, his booming voice echoed through D Block and into the main cell house. "This is the associate warden! Throw down your weapons and surrender! You are completely surrounded and cannot get out of the cell house! You have nothing to gain by continuing! Come out in the open with your hands up, and you will not be shot!"

Silence.

Inside the gun galleries, the officers peered into the darkened cell house for any sign of activity. In their cells, the D Block inmates welcomed the respite from the barrage and listened for a response. The convicts in the main cell house waited silently for the drama to play out. On the catwalk Miller listened for a response, sure the rioters would not answer.

From somewhere inside the cell house, Hubbard yelled, "Come and get us, you motherfuckers!"

Miller shook his head in disgust. He knew it. The convicts would never surrender. They would have to be taken by force. But when he reported to Warden Johnston, the warden was still unyielding.

"Well, that's too bad, Mr. Miller. We'll have to think about this some more. I'll get right back with you." Johnston turned his attention to a pile of papers on his desk, pointedly ignoring his assistant.

From makeshift bunkers on the hill below the cell house, the barrage continued. Rotating teams of officers and Marines fired relentlessly into the D Block windows. The bullets sprayed the top tier of cells. The gas shells that sliced through the barred windows created a tear-gas hell for the prisoners in D Block and the guards in the gallery. Tracer bullets added to the drama of the bombardment, particularly for the crowds watching from the distant shores.

In the east gun gallery, Cochanour and Mullen, stiff and aching from hours of crouching on their hands and knees, maintained a silent vigil, peering into the semidarkness of the cell house. In the west gallery, Bergen and the others periodically fired blindly at the D Block cells. In response to Bergen's demands that they surrender, the D Block inmates shouted back that there were no weapons in D Block and that no one in D Block was involved in the break. Their denials fell on deaf ears. The barrage continued.

When the escape attempt began, nine inmate patients were in the prison hospital under the care of Dr. Stuart Clark, a young Public Health Service physician substituting for the regular prison doctor. Also present were the prison dentist making his weekly visit, a medical technician, and Glen Pehrson, the regularly assigned hospital custodial officer.

When they realized the gravity of the situation, Pehrson and the others considered ways to protect themselves and the inmates from possible invasion by the rioters. The two medical men immediately thought of a solution. They mixed a preparation of plaster of paris and carefully packed it into the door lock. In minutes it was dry, permanently freezing the lock and sealing the door shut. Behind the sealed door, the occupants of the hospital waited for the revolt to end.

In cells 402 and 403, the hostages anxiously awaited rescue. They heard Coy, Cretzer, and Hubbard talking in the utility corridor. Death lurked literally around the corner. Lageson and Burdett continued to minister to the unconscious Weinhold, furnishing him water and adjusting his position to relieve his stiffening muscles. Miller and Corwin remained silent. Simpson appeared to be in a coma. Baker waivered in and out of consciousness.

At 10:45 P.M., Warden Johnston entered the associate warden's office. Miller was behind his desk, gulping coffee and wrestling with how to convince Johnston to authorize a rescue mission. Miller looked up, not knowing what to expect from Johnston.

The older man looked haggard and drawn. "Well, Mr. Miller, do you still wish to lead an assault team into the cell house?" Johnston asked without expression.

"Yes, Sir, Warden. I do."

"Very well. Do you have in mind the men you will take with you as part of this detail?"

"Yes, Sir," Miller said, and detailed the plan he had been thinking about for hours. "There will be ten of us, including Lieutenants Faulk and Roberts as well as a number of other senior men. We intend to enter through the main gate and go down past the library between C Block and D Block. We believe the hostages are in the west end of the cell house, probably somewhere in C Block."

"Very well, Mr. Miller. Good luck to you. Keep me advised." The weary old man walked slowly out the door and into the safe haven of his office.

Miller's group was eager. Each man was armed and carried several pouches of ammunition. Most carried Winchester riot guns, five-shot shotguns capable of producing an expansive cloud of buckshot. Three of the men, including Miller, carried automatic pistols in their waistbands. Miller assembled the crew and outlined his plan. They would go in through the main gate and make their way down Seedy Street. The men with the riot guns would be responsible for protecting the group against gunfire from the tops of the cell blocks. The men with the handguns also carried flashlights and were to search each cell as they moved along.

Finally, more than nine hours after the uprising had begun, Associate Warden Miller lead the assault he felt should have been undertaken immediately. Miller and Officers Donald Maury and Roy Sievertson led the way. The group entered the cell house, moved slowly across the east end to Seedy Street, then headed west. They crept along the empty corridor, hugging the south wall. Most of the lights had been turned off to protect the rescue party, and the cell house was almost dark. The men with the riot guns formed a perimeter around the group, all with their guns pointed at the ceiling, scanning the upper tiers for lurking convicts. No one spoke.

As they passed the library, a voice called out of the darkness. "Hey, Mr. Miller, there's two of us in here. We're not involved in this thing."

Miller recognized the voice and called out. "Cook, who's in there with you?"

"Dub Baker is in here," he responded. "And neither one of us had anything to do with this."

"Come out of there with your hands up and stand out here in front of us," Miller demanded.

"Okay, we're coming, don't shoot. We're not involved." The two frightened convicts followed the associate warden's orders and hurried through the unlocked library door with their hands raised high above their heads. They stood in the middle of Seedy Street, illuminated by flashlight beams. Miller jammed his pistol into his waistband and searched the two inmates, then pushed them into a nearby empty cell. As he did, he heard Sundstrom at the west end of the corridor shout out, "Hey, we're down here! Hey, here we are!" Looking down the darkened aisle, Miller caught sight of a towel waving out of one of the cells. They had found the hostages.

The rescue party hustled down the aisle toward the flapping towel. Just then, a shot rang out. A bullet crashed into the wire-mesh wall of the library above their heads. The shooter retreated as the seven officers with riot guns opened fire, pouring buckshot all along the top of C Block. Through the staccato of the barrage, Sundstrom shouted, "They're up on top of C Block. Don't come down any further this way. Go around the other way. We've got several wounded men down here."

"We're coming!" Miller shouted. "Hang on, you guys, we'll get you out of there in a minute. In the meantime, we'll blast the hell out of these goddam cons."

The entire detail withdrew to the east end of the cell house. From there they moved methodically down Michigan Boulevard, illuminating each main-floor cell with flashlights as they went, satisfying themselves there were no gunmen hiding. Working their way along B Block, they reached the west end of the cell house. At the end of B Block, the officers with riot guns sent a ferocious broadside into the top of C Block while Miller and Faulk made their way around the end of C Block to the hostage cells. Throwing open the doors, they discovered the cells full of wounded guards.

Stretchers were brought in and the five critically wounded men were removed. Bristow, Burdett, Sundstrom, and Lageson assisted in the rescue of the more seriously wounded. It was a slow, tedious process, carried out under the protective barrage of the riflemen. As the last hostage was carried out, Faulk locked the door to D Block. The rescue was a success!

The celebration was tempered, however, by concern for the five wounded men. Since the prison hospital was sealed off, the island medical staff could render only basic first aid. The injured men needed to be moved to the dock and transported to a hospital on the mainland as soon as possible.

The uninjured hostages immediately made themselves available for duty. Bristow set up a makeshift kitchen and began preparing sandwiches and coffee. Sundstrom, Burdett, and Lageson presented themselves to the armory to draw weapons and join the next assault team entering the cell house. But they were denied weapons and directed by the associate warden to perform noncombatant duties in the office areas instead.

"Jesus, Ernie, you look terrible, you better have that face looked at," Miller said.

"I think I look a lot worse than I am. What I'd really like is a .45 automatic and the chance to go back in there after those bastards. You don't look so good yourself, Ed," Lageson replied, gesturing at the associate warden's burned and swollen face.

"Oh, this is no big deal," Miller responded, minimizing his injury. "I just got in the way of an exploding gas billy."

Lageson finally sat down. He was exhausted. His first thoughts were of Eunice and Ernie. He knew how worried they would be. He jumped to his feet and headed for the phone to call home.

"Ernie! Ernie! Wake up, Son! Dad's okay!"

Through his sleepy haze, Ernie Jr. saw his mother silhouetted against the hall light. It was nearly midnight. He had been in a restless fit of sleep, but the news jolted him awake. The horrifying experience was over. He sat up and hugged his mother.

23

The euphoria caused by the rescue was short lived. Though all the hostages were now accounted for, three of them—Weinhold, Simpson, and Corwin—were gravely wounded. Miller and Baker were also badly injured, but their conditions didn't appear to be as serious. All five, as well as Fred Roberts, who had received a minor wound to the back during the rescue, were taken to Marine Hospital in San Francisco.

The warden came out of his office when he heard the hostages had been rescued. He circulated among those involved, congratulating the assault team and attempting to comfort the wounded hostages. The deep lines in his face and the anguish in his eyes signaled his fatigue and psychological agony. One of his men was dead and fifteen were wounded, five severely. And the struggle for control of his prison was far from over, with at least three armed prisoners still at large in the cell house. He knew that the associate warden and lieutenants would soon be contacting him regarding the future course of action. Sadly, he had no ideas.

His rounds of congratulations and greetings over, Johnston again sought the protection of his office as he pondered what lay ahead. He slumped in his chair, totally exhausted. He spun around to face the wall, hands folded on his chest. As he stared at the diplomas and certificates of award covering his office walls, thoughts raced through his mind. He didn't know what to do next. Truthfully, he hoped his assistant would have a suggestion. He wondered how the Marines could help. He swore to himself that he would do nothing to endanger the lives of any more of his men. His thoughts were interrupted by a knock on his office door and the presence of the associate warden in the doorway.

"Come in, Ed," he said, with more warmth than Miller had heard in his voice all day. "Bring me up to date on the status of things."

"It's possible there's one man in D Block, maybe Cretzer. If so, he's totally pinned down in there because Faulk locked the D Block door when we got the hostages out." Miller went on to explain that part of the Marine weapon team was still on the hill below the cell house firing rifles and grenades into D Block. "Our people have been firing into D Block since mid-afternoon. At about 7:00, the Marines set up a team down there with us. The last report we had from Bergen in the west gallery was that there hasn't been any hostile fire from D Block in quite some time, so we might want to consider knocking off the shelling. We might also consider sending an assault team into D Block. If there are any holdouts in there, it sure wouldn't be hard to go in and get the bastards out.

"We're pretty sure some or all of them are in the C Block utility corridor. The hostages heard them talking in there, and the rescue party was fired at by someone on the top of C Block. All three of them may be in there. Shockley, Carnes, and Thompson have all been seen back in their cells, so that leaves only Coy, Cretzer, and Hubbard unaccounted for. They've got no way out. We think the best way to go would be to storm the corridor and just blast them out. We could go in with shotguns and rifles, or we could use some of the fancy stuff the Marines have. They've got grenades and flamethrowers. They've even got a bazooka."

Listening to Miller, Warden Johnston's spirits lifted. Things were not as hopeless as he had thought. He still didn't want to jeopardize any more of his men, however, so he vetoed Miller's suggestion of an armed assault.

"It's just too dangerous, Ed. Those men in there are armed and probably prepared to fight to the death. I don't want any of our people put in a position of danger. Let's get that Marine, Mr. Buckner, in here to see if he has any ideas."

The detachment of Marines was led by thirty-two-

year-old Warrant Officer Charles Buckner. A native
of Memphis, Tennessee, Buckner was a hero of
hard-fought campaigns on the Pacific islands of
Guam and Bougainville. On Guam he led a force
that stopped a Japanese Bonzai charge and was instrumental in capturing the island. Buckner was an
expert in special weapons. He had been awarded
the Silver Star and the Purple Heart. He was a self-
assured, cocky young officer, supremely confident of
his ability to quell what he viewed as a minor prison
disturbance. Buckner was exactly what Johnston was
looking for.

At midnight, Buckner met with Miller and
Johnston to outline a plan of action. Buckner had
decided that the rioters could be subdued by gas and
fragmentation grenades. He assured the warden that
with the weapons at his disposal, he could bring the
riot to an end without further risk of injury to the
custodial force. He warned that he would probably
kill the convicts but promised to end the holdout.

"I don't care if they get killed or not," Johnston
responded. "They're three useless lives at this point.
They've been given the opportunity to surrender and
have chosen to dig in and fight. As far as I'm concerned, if they get killed, so be it. But I don't want
any custodial officers hurt, and I don't want any of
those convicts out of that corridor with guns in their
hands."

"We'll get them, Warden! We'll get them with the
fragmentation and concussion grenades. They won't
stand a chance. It'll be messy and we'll break up
your jail, but I can promise you three very dead

convicts when this thing is over. Nobody's coming out of there alive."

"Mr. Buckner, I like your style," Warden Johnston said, smiling. "Go ahead and blast the bastards."

Buckner needed information about the physical layout of the cell blocks and the utility corridor. From the blueprints of the prison, Buckner concluded that the ventilating system offered a straight shot from the roof to where Coy, Cretzer, and Hubbard were holed up. The Marines would drop gas and fragmentation grenades through the ventilating system into the corridor below.

With the help of Sievertson and a couple of other officers, Buckner carried several cases of hand grenades to the cell-house roof. They first dropped a number of gas grenades down the ventilator shafts. Choking gas spewed throughout the small space. Expecting such an attack, the convicts immediately donned their gas masks.

After the meeting with Buckner, Johnston sent his fifth message to the press:

> *We have been able to rescue several officers who were hostages. Lt. Joseph Simpson shot several times in the stomach, condition critical. R.R. Baker shot in the legs, very serious. Capt. Henry H. Weinhold shot, critical condition. Cecil D. Corwin, critical condition. William A. Miller, very serious condition. Carl W. Sundstrom, Record Clerk, was shot at but not hit. Joseph Burdett, Ernest B. Lageson, Robert C. Bristow, Fred S. Roberts, slightly wounded.*

*Prisoners who led in assaults are Coy, Cretzer,
Thompson, Shockley, Fleish, Carnes. Three officers who are critically wounded say they were
shot by Joseph Paul Cretzer, #548AZ, who is
under life sentence for murder of U.S. Marshal
at Tacoma, when he was on trial for escape
from McNeil Island to which prison he had
been sentenced for numerous bank robberies.*

At 12:30 A.M., a relief detachment of Marines arrived, bringing with them twenty-four cases of
SHAPE bombs. These new military explosives were
designed to penetrate concrete bunkers and had
proved effective against the Japanese during the Pacific campaign. In addition, the Marines carried ba-
zookas, flamethrowers, and light machine guns. Several hundred fragmentation and concussion grenades
were delivered from the military arsenal at Benicia,
California.

As the night wore on, the bombardment esca-
lated. The crowds of onlookers maintained their vigil
all night long. High-intensity searchlights from the
towers and ships off-shore illuminated the entire
south side of the cell house. A bazooka emplace-
ment was established, but the warden rejected the
use of such a powerful weapon. He feared the explosive force of the weapon could not be controlled
and feared for the safety of the guards occupying the
west gun gallery. The glass had been blown out of
the D Block windows, permitting the chill, damp
wind off the bay to swirl through the cell block. The
continuous shelling made it impossible for the D

Block inmates to move around in their cells. Most of them lay on the floor behind piles of mattresses, pillows, and books. In addition to the grenades, hundreds of rifle-and-machine gun bullets poured through the broken windows, striking mainly the upper tier of cells. Periodically the deck guns of one of the Coast Guard cutters fired, sending huge projectiles screaming into the embattled isolation cell block.

In the cramped spaces of the C Block utility corridor, the morale of the holdouts was deteriorating. When Cretzer had recklessly gunned down the men in the hostage cells, he had felt a sadistic pleasure in pumping slugs into Weinhold and Simpson and considered their deaths to be his legacy to the prisoner population. But from what he had heard of the rescue, it was obvious that all the hostages were alive. Everything associated with the breakout had been a failure. Having had nine chances and having failed miserably, Cretzer now wanted to kill at least one guard.

Cornered as they were, all three inmates knew that it was only a matter of time until they were overwhelmed. Coy and Cretzer would be ready for the attack. They were armed. But Hubbard had only a knife and a couple of billy clubs. The three concealed themselves below the floorboards, protected by the darkness of the corridor and prepared to fight to the end, even through the clouds of tear gas.

The exploding hand grenades presented an unexpected problem for Cretzer and his mates. "What the fuck is that?" Cretzer asked Coy when the first fragmentation grenade rattled down the ventilator shaft and exploded with deafening force at the end of the corridor. They were unaware that the Marines were involved and assumed the prison officials were using dynamite. The wood floorboards protected the men from all but the sound and concussive force of the explosions. Concealed as they were, however, in the bottom of the corridor, they couldn't even fire back. They had to wait for an attack. Throughout the night they endured the periodic blasts and continuous gas bombing.

With the first light of day, Miller and Officer Ray Spencer joined Buckner and Sievertson on the cellhouse roof with equipment to drill concrete. The men plotted various points on the roof that were above areas of the corridor not yet subjected to the grenade pounding. They then drilled five holes through the concrete roof. With this, Buckner felt confident he would be able to blanket the entire corridor with a lethal spray of shrapnel.

24

The approximately twenty-five prisoners still in their cells in C Block were taking a merciless beating from the Marine barrage. The concrete walls protected them from the white-hot shrapnel, but the sounds, fumes, and bone-jarring concussions were unbearable. Late Friday morning, all the C Block inmates were moved from their cells into empty cells in B Block. The inmate work crews, who had spent the night in the yard, were brought in and housed in A and B Blocks.

For most of these inmates, it was now a festive occasion. Once in their new cells, protected by the anonymity provided by the confusion and chaotic conditions, they began shouting at the Marines and the guards and voicing encouragement to the hold-outs in the utility corridor.

"Hey, Jughead, how about getting us some chow

up here. We ain't had anything to eat since yesterday."

"How many of you screws have been shot up so far? I hope it's plenty."

"Hang in there, you guys. Nail a screw for me."

Once all the inmates were relocated, they were served sandwiches and coffee. The men had gone more than twenty-four hours without food, and the spartan meal provoked more abusive shouting and jeering catcalls. The inmates were also given mattresses, blankets, and some items for personal hygiene. Then the officers withdrew from the cell house, and the mind-numbing bombardment of the utility corridor resumed. The merciless firing into D Block, unaffected by the relocation of the inmates in the main cell house, continued unabated throughout the day.

At Marine Hospital in San Francisco, a team of surgeons worked frantically to save the lives of the wounded officers. Weinhold and Simpson were the most seriously injured and received priority in the operating room. Weinhold had been shot at close range in the chest. Simpson had similar wounds in the chest and abdomen. Both men withstood the surgery well but remained in critical condition. Corwin, although suffering serious injuries, was not in a life-threatening state. Surgical repair of his shattered jaw and grossly deforming facial wound was delayed until the condition of the other two men had stabilized.

Bill Miller, the youngest of the seriously wounded, appeared to be in the best condition, so surgical intervention to repair his wounds was also delayed. As he lay on a gurney awaiting his turn in surgery, he suffered massive internal bleeding, particularly in the area of the lungs. He went into shock and died at 6:30 on Friday morning. Some of the reporters covering the story inquired whether earlier treatment of Miller could have saved his life, but neither prison authorities nor hospital personnel would comment.

When they were brought to the hospital, all four men signed deathbed declarations. They were advised of the critical nature of their wounds and that they may not survive. At the request of the U.S. Attorney's office, each of the four men signed the following declaration:

> *Being in a critical condition and believing that I am now dying, I make this my sworn statement. That I was shot with a .45 Colt revolver by Joseph Cretzer, #548AZ, whom I can positively identify. Joseph Cretzer shot me cold bloodedly and said, "I will kill you." Cretzer shot me when I was in a cell in which he and other prisoners had placed me.*

With all the convicts removed from C Block, Buckner stepped up his attack. The holes in the roof had been drilled, so he was able to increase the tempo of the barrage. For a time he fired rifle gre nades into the corridor, aiming at as many parts of the space as he could. He then devised a method of suspending each grenade with a length of string to position the explosive a measured distance above the floor of the corridor. A second string tied to the firing pin allowed him to detonate the grenade at selected heights. By swinging the grenades back and forth as he exploded them, he was able to insure complete explosive coverage of the entire corridor, blasting a deadly hail of shrapnel into every square foot of the enclosed space.

The force of the grenades ruptured the sewer lines, and raw sewage spilled into the corridor. The blasts also shattered the saltwater lines that fed the toilets, releasing hundreds of gallons of sea water into the confined area. Steam and freshwater lines were ripped open and electrical lines shredded. After several hours of bombing, the corridor became a twisted mess of steel beams and broken concrete, mired in a pool of raw sewage and salt water.

Driven from the passageway, the three battered convicts retreated into a tunnel under the floor of the cutoff. Here, wedged in a concrete cocoon, they were safe from the shrapnel but not from the ear-splitting sounds and body-wrenching concussions of the explosions. All three had been hit by shrapnel, although none of their wounds were serious.

Buckner pored over the blueprints. He suspected that the inmates would take refuge in the tunnel. Buckner attacked this location with antitank grenades and SHAPE bombs. The explosive force was devastating, but even the finest weapons of the U.S.

military could not penetrate the floor of the Alcatraz cell house.

In time, however, the tunnel became unbearable for Coy, Cretzer, and Hubbard. The shock waves numbed their bodies, each concussion like being hit by a pile driver. Even worse, the confined space began to fill with water and raw sewage. They had to make their way out of the tunnel and into the south half of the corridor. All three were bleeding from shrapnel wounds. Their heads pounded. The ringing in their ears prevented any conversation. Each man stationed himself between a pair of cross beams, sitting in the filth on the corridor floor. They were able to crouch between the beams with only the tops of their heads showing above the floor-boards. The three waited, weapons in hand, for the onslaught they knew would come.

25

The Marine-and prison-guard cannonade of D Block continued until mid-afternoon. Marine grenades and guard rifle-fire poured through the broken windows. From inside, they could hear the screams of the begging convicts.

"You're killing us!" came the repeated plea. "Let us out of here, you fucking killers!"

Much of the gunfire raked the area of cells 41 and 42 at the east end of D Block on the upper tier. The prisoners had a theory as to why this was the case. Robert Stroud occupied cell 42. It was his opinion, and that of many other convicts, that the shelling was directed at him personally. Stroud was viewed by prison authorities as a troublemaker. His national reputation as an expert on bird diseases and author of the definitive volume on the subject brought him a great deal of attention. While prison authorities attempted to limit his privileges and influence, his fans on the outside constantly lobbied for his transfer. Stroud's activities were severely limited when he was transferred to The Rock. He was denied the right to keep birds in his cell or anywhere in the prison, a privilege he had enjoyed at Leavenworth. No exceptions to the correspondence regulations were made for him, so outsiders could no longer seek his advice or access his knowledge and expertise. Visitation restrictions prevented anyone from seeing him. As a result, Warden Johnston received considerable criticism for suppressing academic freedom, despite the fact that Stroud was a double murderer, with one victim a Leavenworth prison guard.

The men of D Block also believed that the prolonged shelling of the isolation cells was an act of revenge for the death and injury inflicted on the custodial force by the rioters. There had been no hostile gunfire from D Block since 7:00 Thursday evening. The door between isolation and the main cell house had been locked since the hostage rescue. The convicts believed that since the officers in the gun gallery were safe behind the steel shield mounted in the front of the gallery, the guards and Marines were firing with impunity from below as retribution for Cretzer's murderous conduct.

Finally, late in the day Friday, Stroud dashed from his cell and took refuge in the first cell at the west end. From there he negotiated with Bergen in the gun gallery to bring the shooting to an end. He pleaded repeatedly for the shooting to stop, arguing that there were no weapons or hostile inmates in D Block. As proof of this, he offered himself as a human shield for any officer who wished to enter D Block and search each cell individually. In response to the offer, Bergen called the warden, who agreed to terminate the bombardment. D Block finally fell silent.

The interior of the utility corridor had been totally destroyed. Shattered steam lines hissed. Live electrical lines dangled from the narrow passage walls. The stench was overpowering. Warrant Officer Buckner insisted that no one could have survived and asked the warden to discontinue the bombardment. Warden Johnston thanked Buckner and released the Marines.

Back on the mainland, the tired Marine officer spoke to the press, likening his experience to those he'd had while fighting the Japanese on Bougainville and Guam. "It was like cleaning out those tunnels and pillboxes occupied by the Japs. We had some tough assignments out there, but take it from me, Alcatraz Island Prison is the toughest defensive position I ever saw. Buckner estimated that he dropped at least 500 hand grenades, admitting that his intention was to riddle the area where the cons were hiding. "If there's any cons left in C Block, they're sure as hell dead cookies by now," he said.

After the withdrawal of the Marines, the custodial force continued firing into the corridor until the early evening. One officer opened the door to the corridor while everyone stood clear. Other officers then took turns emptying their weapons into the dark passageway. Then the door was closed and locked. There was never any return fire from within.

In D Block, the water and steam lines had also been severed, and the entire block was flooded. The area was littered with shattered glass, explosive debris, and an array of dud shells and unexploded projectiles. The explosive devices had showered hot shrapnel into the cells, starting several fires. These fires had smoldered, filling D Block with smoke, until they were extinguished by the flooding water. The D Block inmates were all thankful. They were alive. It was finally over.

Outside the utility corridor on Friday night, a day and a half after Coy had begun the escape attempt by overpowering the yard-door guard, the officers stood by for orders from the warden to storm in and take the holdouts. It had been at least two hours since they had last fired into the corridor. The general consensus among the guards was that the convicts inside were dead.

Suddenly a single shot rang out from inside the corridor. A bullet tore through the east door. The slug passed inches above the head of Joe Steere and splattered into lead droplets against the cell-house wall. This brought a renewed round of firing into the corridor. Officers took turns firing volleys into the darkness. There was no response from inside. After this process was repeated two or three times over the next few hours, the doors at both ends of the corridor were closed and locked.

Associate Warden Miller shook his head in disgust. That single shot would cost them hours and hours as Warden Johnston vacillated.

The night was calm. The exhausted custodial force was finally able to rest. The prisoner population, too, was able to rest for the first time in two days, free from the ear-splitting barrage of grenades, bombs, and bullets. Bristow and a group of volunteers turned out hundreds of sandwiches and gallons of hot coffee for the weary guards and prisoners.

The quiet lull was a refreshing time, but Warden Johnston and his men knew that the final chapter of the episode was yet to be played out. Ahead lay the final entry into the corridor and either a shoot-out with the surviving members of the escape attempt or the recovery of their bodies.

26

Early Saturday morning, after two sleepless nights, Warden Johnston stared, red-eyed, out his office window. At 8:00, he received an urgent phone call from Oakland criminal lawyer Leo Sullivan. Sullivan was well known to Johnston. He had represented a number of Alcatraz inmates over the years.

"Warden, Leo Sullivan here. I'm calling from home with what might be some significant help for you in resolving the riot. I realize your situation out there is a little precarious, and I wouldn't be bothering you if I didn't think I could help."

"Well, things are pretty well under control out here, Leo," Johnston responded. "But what is it you have in mind that you think will help?"

Sullivan went on to explain that late Friday night he had been contacted by a woman introducing herself first as Kay Wallace, then admitting to be Kay Benedetti, the former wife of Joe Cretzer. She advised Sullivan that although she had divorced Cretzer and renounced her former lifestyle, she wanted to help prevent any further bloodshed, if she could. She volunteered to go to Alcatraz and plead with Cretzer to give up the escape attempt and surrender. She asked that her proposal remain anonymous, but she was willing to meet with Cretzer even if her identity was revealed to the press.

Johnston thanked Sullivan for the offer and asked the attorney to convey his thanks to Mrs. Benedetti for her willingness to help. He explained there was no way to reach Cretzer, who had rejected all efforts to negotiate. Under the circumstances, Johnston advised, there was nothing Mrs. Benedetti or anyone else could do.

Leaning back in his chair, Johnston realized Miller's recommendations had been right all along. An armed assault on the utility corridor was the only alternative. He called Miller's office and told his associate warden, "Ed, do whatever you have to do to get those cons out of the corridor." Hanging up the phone, he made yet another trip to the toilet.

Miller called for volunteers to go into the C Block utility corridor. Every officer present raised his hand to go. He randomly selected Joe Steere, Ray Spencer, and Don Mowery. Considering the danger involved, Miller questioned each of the three individually, making sure they understood the magnitude of the risk and offering them an opportunity to change their minds. No, absolutely not. They were all anxious to go.

At 9:00 on Saturday morning, the three officers entered the east end of the dark corridor. With the others positioned outside the line of fire, Miller opened the door and quickly stood aside. The group waited in silence for several seconds, but no sound came from inside. "Okay, Don, go on in," Miller ordered. "But be goddam careful."

Mowery stepped cautiously through the doorway, shining the beam of light from his huge flashlight into the corridor ahead of him. He waited, holding his breath, then moved slowly through the twisted pipes, wire, and debris. The moist air reeked. Water still dripped from the ruptured pipes. He directed his light along the floorboards. Twenty or twenty-five feet into the corridor, he saw what appeared to be the top of a man's head. Stepping carefully over the splintered planks, he focused his light. The water and floating debris were nearly a foot deep.

Mowery called over his shoulder to Spencer, who was two paces behind with his machine gun cocked. "Cover me, Spence. That's Coy up ahead. He looks dead." Mowery moved swiftly to the body and positively identified it as that of Bernie Coy. Still clad in Weinhold's uniform jacket, Coy was in a sitting position facing Mowery. His arms rested on a cross beam, holding the rifle in a firing position, with his right index finger wrapped around the trigger. Mowery saw bullet holes in the dead convict's head and dried blood caked on the right side of his face. Mowery retrieved the rifle. As he did, he could tell that the body was in an advanced state of rigor mortis. "Here Spence, pass this back," Mowery whispered as he handed the wet gun to his fellow officer. Moving broken pipes and dangling wires aside, he stepped over Coy's stiff body and continued his grisly journey down the unlighted passageway.

The beam of his flashlight next illuminated the body of Marv Hubbard. Hubbard was seated a few feet beyond Coy, facing in the opposite direction, with a large butcher knife beside him. A significant portion of his head was missing, and his face was covered with blood. His body was still warm, indicating he had not been dead for more than a few hours. Mowery picked up the knife and, without comment, handed it over his shoulder to Spencer.

Fifteen or twenty feet further into the corridor, Mowery observed Cretzer's crouching body facing him. His eyes were wide open in death. He wore an officer's uniform jacket and held an automatic pistol in his right hand. His arm was flexed, with the pistol in a firing position. The barrel of the pistol was pointed downward, as though Cretzer had eased his grip on the gun as he died. Mowery jerked the pistol from the dead convict's stiffened hand. Passing it back to Spencer, Mowery declared with relief, "Let's get the hell out of here! I can't stand this stink any longer."

The bodies were laid out on stretchers along the east wall of the cell house and prepared for shipment to the San Francisco morgue. Bergen, with assistance from Mowery and Frank Delling, a mortician before joining the prison service, attended to this morbid task. The bodies were disrobed and wrapped in blankets. Then the clothing was searched. Coy's pockets contained fourteen rifle shells and cell-house keys with the numbers 111, 103N, and 107. Key 111 was to the door between the cell house and the dining hall. 103N was to the door of the C Block utility corridor. Displaying key 107 to Delling and Mowery, Bergen said, "Well, Bernie had the right key, but I guess he couldn't make it work. He never got any closer to San Francisco than when he was making magazine deliveries to D Block."

With the bodies of the dead convicts removed, Miller turned his attention to D Block. No gunfire or hostile activity had been observed from any of the cells for over forty hours. D Block had been under the constant scrutiny of the officers in the west gallery since 7:00 P.M. Thursday. The prisoners in D Block had repeatedly assured Bergen that there were no weapons there and that none of the D Block inmates were involved in the uprising. Despite all this evidence, Miller had lingering doubts about security in D Block.

For the entry into D Block, Miller assembled a team of more than a dozen armed officers. Weary from lack of sleep, several of the men were tense and skittish, and all of them were ready to fire at the least provocation. In their cells, the prisoners, who had gone without sleep or food for two days, waited fearfully for the next step in the deadly drama. They feared the worst when the door from the cell house opened and they heard Miller's voice. They believed that the two-day bombardment had been an attempt by prison officials to inflict death and injury on all those confined in isolation. Even the most hardened among the group were fearful of what would happen with the arrival of the custodial force.

The associate warden picked his way gingerly through the field of unexploded shells and grenades that littered the floor and positioned himself in the middle of the block, facing the cells. A dozen officers, all armed with shotguns and rifles, stationed themselves along the wall behind him and stood motionless under the blackened, blown-out windows. The officers held their weapons in firing positions, aimed directly at the prisoners, most of whom had retreated to the back of their cells.

"All right, you men, listen to my instructions and listen good," Miller's booming voice echoed. "I'm only going to say this once. You're going to do exactly as you're told and keep your mouths shut. These guns behind me are loaded. If any of you get the least bit out of line, you get shot. Nobody says a word. Do exactly as you are told.

"I want each of you to step forward and stick your hands through the bars of your cell door as far as you can and stand in that position until your name is called and your cell door is opened. When your name is called and your door opens, you are to step out onto the tier, remove all your clothes, including shoes and socks, and drop everything over the rail down onto the flats. Then put your hands over the rail and lean forward over the rail and stand there without moving. You and your cell will then be searched, your cell will be stripped, and you will be permitted to go back into your cell. Anybody who moves or pulls anything fancy gets his ass blown off."

Not a sound came from any of the cells. The convicts adhered strictly to Miller's instructions. Miller seemed to them a different man. Even when he meted out punishment or shouted at an inmate before, there had always been an element of humanity in his demeanor. Today his voice was devoid of any trace of compassion. His manner was threatening and full of rage. And all those guns! The D Block cons were no fools. They didn't complain.

"All right! Move!" Miller barked. The convicts moved to the front of their cells, thrust their arms through the bars of their cell doors, and stood silently as ordered. One by one, the names of the inmates were called, starting with Robert Stroud. Stroud's cell door was opened by an officer operating the cell-control mechanism at the opposite end of the tier. The door clanged open. Stroud stepped cautiously out of his cell. Two unarmed guards approached the inmate as he disrobed. As he stood naked leaning over the rail of the tier, the chill wind coming off the bay caused the aging convict to shiver. His cell was thoroughly searched. His clothing, linens, and mattress were thrown over the rail onto the floor two levels below. His personal items, papers, books, and notes were piled in the rear corner of his cell. He was searched, then ordered back into his cell. The next name was called. This procedure was repeated until all the prisoners and cells on the top tier had been searched. The middle-tier cells and inmates were then searched, and after that the bottom tier was secured. Securing D Block took three hours.

Once the block was secure, Miller and his men withdrew, leaving the naked inmates locked in their cells with only their bare steel bunks, sinks and toilets. The fear and tension among the convicts was so great that even after the associate warden and his search party departed, the silence continued. From the gun gallery, the armed officers continued to watch over the cells and their occupants.

Immediately after the search party left, a crew of Navy demolition experts carefully inspected the entire cell block. They gathered up all the unexploded shells and grenades and removed them from the building.

Miller's next task was to isolate the three surviving insurgents from the rest of the prisoner population. Accompanied by three armed officers, Miller stormed back into D Block and dragged the naked Shockley from his cell. "Get out of there, you glass-eyed son of a bitch," Miller ordered, as two of the officers pulled the frightened convict from his cell onto the debris-littered tier. Herded along the tier and down the steps to the main floor, the terrified Shockley suffered cuts to the bottoms of his feet as he stepped on jagged shards of glass and steel. Shockley was taken to A Block and pushed into a cell. The door slammed behind him. Carnes and Thompson were also taken from their cells, stripped, and searched. All their personal belongings and clothing were stripped from their cells and thrown into the corridor. Both men were pushed and kicked along by the associate warden to cells near Shockley.

Miller interrogated each of the three separately, demanding to know the names of all the participants, periodically punching and kicking the cowering convicts.

Before the end of the day, all the D Block inmates had been fed and permitted to shower. Blankets, sheets, clean uniforms, towels, and basic personal-hygiene products were supplied to them as well. They welcomed the simplest of creature comforts.

27

It was early afternoon on Saturday when Ernie Lageson Sr. finally returned to his Sacramento Street apartment. He had remained on duty on the island without sleep continuously since his rescue late Thursday night. By Saturday afternoon, however, Lageson was exhausted. He looked it.

When the lobby bell in the apartment sounded, Ernie Jr. leapt to his feet and ran to the apartment door. "Mom! It's Dad! He's home!" Throwing open the door, he ran into the hall and looked down the three flights of stairs to see his father in the lobby.

"Dad! Dad! Are you okay?"

"Yes, Son," his father called from below. "Everything's great. Boy, am I happy to be home!"

Eunice was shocked at the sight of her husband as he walked in the door. The left side of his face was badly swollen and discolored. He wore a bandage on his cheek and carried a three-day growth of beard. His eyes were dark and sunken. The lines in his face showed the strain and torment he had been through.

They lovingly embraced as young Ernie stood quietly in the background. "Oh, Ernie," Eunice whispered. "I'm so glad to have you back. This has been the worst time of my life."

"You know, Sweetie," he smiled, "it hasn't been one of my better times either."

They smiled and held one another, tears trickling down their cheeks. Releasing her embrace, Eunice stepped aside.

The youngster rushed to his father. He kissed the man's tear-stained face and hugged him around the neck. "Boy, Dad, I was really scared. I was afraid that you wouldn't come home. Was it terrible?"

"It was pretty bad for a while, Son. And it's sure nothing I ever want to go through again. I'll tell you, Pal, I sure did a lot of praying last Thursday night. I guess someone heard me."

"Can I get you something to eat, Honey?" Eunice asked. "You look like you could use a good meal."

"You know, I'm too tired to eat. What I'd really like to do is lie down. Let's all go into the bedroom. I'll spread out on the bed, and you guys can ask me questions till I fall asleep."

"I want to hear all about it, Dad. Let's go!"

Eunice really didn't want to hear all about it, but to do so was a small price to pay for having the nightmare over and her husband home. As Lageson lay wearily on the bed, removing nothing but his jacket and shoes, his son bombarded him with questions.

28

With much fanfare the press was told that Warden James Johnston and James V. Bennett, director of the Federal Bureau of Prisons, would hold a news conference in the warden's office on Saturday evening. The announcement caused a stir within the local press corps. This would be the first press conference ever conducted on Alcatraz and the first time that the press would be permitted to set foot on the island.

For security reasons, the prison administration had always maintained a low news profile to prevent disclosure of Alcatraz procedures and practices. But the recent events had captured the attention of the entire nation, and misinformation was being circulated by the news media. Government officials were demanding to know what had happened and why. Five men lay dead and sixteen were injured, without explanation. Faced with an overwhelming need to explain his conduct, reveal the facts, and answer his critics, Johnston had little choice but to meet with the press. A special run of the prison launch was scheduled to bring news personnel to the island on Saturday night. The number was limited to one dozen, including representatives of the local newspapers, the news services, the *New York Times*, and Bay-Area radio stations. Included in the group were three photographers, who were permitted to take a limited number of pictures at the warden's discretion.

When the group arrived on the island, they were met by Associate Warden Miller and Lieutenant Ike Faulk, who escorted them to the administration offices and instructed them on the ground rules for the evening. The first phase of the conference would be a tour of the cell house, during which the significant venues would be identified and explained by the warden. The reporters were admonished to stay together, not talk to any inmates, and ask no questions while in the cell house. Following the tour, the group would return to the warden's office, where Warden Johnston would narrate the three-day ordeal. There would then be time for questions. Miller and Faulk warned the newsmen not to overreach. The press conference could be terminated at any time at the discretion of the warden.

The group entered the cell house through the main gate and proceeded down Broadway to Coy's point of entry into the west gun gallery. Here the warden explained how Coy had gained entry to the gallery and overpowered Burch. The group then proceeded to the southwest corner of the cell house, where the warden pointed out the door to D Block, as well as the door to the yard, which the inmates had been unable to open. In the same general area, the hostage cells were identified and described. When the inmates realized that Johnston was leading a tour, they set up a howl of catcalls and obscenities that soon involved the entire prisoner population. The shouting disrupted the warden's tour, and he was visibly disturbed by the commotion. On one occasion during a lull in the shouting, he was hailed by an anonymous voice from a distant cell: "Tell them the truth, you fucking old saltwater bastard!" The comment resonated through the cell house, bringing a new round of laughter and shouts that soon turned into an inmate chant: "Saltwater Johnston! Saltwater Johnston! Saltwater Johnston!"

"Old Salt Water" was a derisive nickname for the warden that the inmates had developed over the years. The origin of the name is now lost, but it was well known to the convicts, the guards, and the warden himself. Unnerved and embarrassed by the conduct of the inmates, Johnston explained the name to the press with a falsehood. "We flushed the place out with salt water a few hours ago," he explained. "I guess the men didn't like it."

The explanation satisfied the reporters but drew smiles from both Miller and Faulk. "Where did that come from?" Faulk inquired of Miller. "He's been 'Old Salt Water' as long as I can remember."

The press corps paused at the east entrance to

the C Block utility corridor. In a theatrical fashion, Johnston told the story of the end of the riot. Flashing a beam of light into the dark corridor, he described the final hours of the uprising. "There, that's where the bastards died like rats in a dirty trench below those pipes. A pretty good foxhole, but we got them." With those remarks the warden concluded the tour.

Following the cell-house tour, the reporters were ushered into the warden's office, where he explained how the escape attempt developed and was subdued. The ordeal had lasted forty-four hours. The warden did all the talking in a manner that discouraged questions. He answered only a few inquiries.

He related an account of Coy's capture of Miller and the other hostages. He began by correctly describing how Coy entered the west gun gallery, overpowered Burch, and returned to the cell-house floor. However, he went on to say that unarmed officers in the cell house rushed Coy as he descended from the gallery but were captured by the armed inmate. Johnston gave no indication that the capture of Weinhold, Simpson, Sundstrom, and Baker had occurred because of confusion within the custodial ranks, which led to the men rushing one or two at a time recklessly into an unknown situation.

A great deal of the information disclosed by Johnston was inconsistent with the facts known to both Miller and Faulk. The two veteran officers were uncomfortable as they listened to the warden speak. He was thoroughly confused about the bar spreader. He told the reporters that it had been fashioned by

Coy at the time of the break from spare plumbing parts he found in the utility corridor. The parts, he claimed, were from the flushing mechanisms of the toilets and were fastened together on the spur of the moment to force the bars apart. He alternately described the device as a crowbar and as a screw jack. The FBI investigation had included a narration of the fabrication of the bar spreader. Hadn't Johnston read it?

Johnston went on with his description of the events of the previous two and a half days, but in Miller's view repeatedly included significant factual misstatements in his account. He said the hostage-rescue team entered the cell house through the yard door. In fact, they entered at the other end of the cell house. He said that his men had regained total control of the cell house and D Block by Thursday evening. In reality, their bombardment went on all day Friday, and the utility corridor was not entered until Saturday morning.

Describing Stites's death, Johnston claimed the officer died entering the gallery through the outside door against heavy inmate gunfire. He claimed that the fatal bullets came from prisoners firing from D Block as Stites was silhouetted against the outside light. The truth was, Stites had been in the gallery for some time and was on the second level. His death occurred as he moved from one section of the gallery to another, while facing the D Block cells. He was silhouetted by light from inside the cell house and was shot in the back by one of his own men firing from outside. Despite irrefutable evidence,

Johnston never admitted that Stites died at the hands of a fellow officer.

As he sat in the corner of the office listening to the warden's inaccurate account of the uprising, Miller whispered to Faulk, "God, Ike, it's like he didn't hear anything I was telling him and hasn't read any of the reports."

"Well, let's face it, Ed. Since he spent most of the time locked in his toilet, it's no wonder he doesn't know what really happened," Faulk said.

Johnston's account of the search for key 107 was also fictional. He claimed that Miller, seeing Coy come at him with the rifle, threw the key into a location where the convict could not find it. Thereafter, Johnston explained, Miller was beaten and tortured by the inmates but doggedly refused to reveal the location of the key. Furious, the inmates shot him in cold blood. "Miller had guts. He threw the key away when he saw Coy coming. We still haven't found that key."

Johnston concluded by setting forth three reasons for the failure of the escape. First he cited Miller's refusal, under torture and beating, to surrender the yard-door key. Second, Johnston claimed, because of the intricate escape-proof electrical locks in the solitary confinement cells, Cretzer was unable to free his co-conspirator, Whitey Franklin. Franklin, the warden explained, was a lock expert whose participation would have made the difference between success and failure. Finally, the warden said, Coy's inability to kill the tower guard caused the break to fail. This reference was presumably to Dock Tower

Officer Comerford, at whom Coy fired from the kitchen.

After the warden finished his lengthy narrative, Director Bennett took center stage and delivered a testimonial in praise of Johnston, perhaps in anticipation of the criticism that would later be leveled at the warden.

"There was not the least indication of negligence or carelessness or inefficiency in this affair. The felons found and took advantage of a weakness which not even the most able and experienced prison man could anticipate. When the emergency broke out, it was handled most courageously, intelligently, and with great devotion to duty. Casualties were kept to a minimum. What was to have been a mass escape failed utterly. Warden Johnston deserves high commendation."

All the observers were not in agreement with Director Bennett's evaluation. Congressman George P. Miller, representative of California's Sixth Congressional District, believed the whole story had not been revealed. He expressed concern as to Johnston's handling of the entire matter. "When I return to Washington I will demand that the Justice Department undertake a full investigation, and if the results are not satisfactory I will call upon Congress to dig to the bottom of this whole affair."

No such investigation was ever undertaken. No official criticism was ever made of Johnston's handling of the uprising.

29

During the three-day Battle of Alcatraz, enormous personal and property damage occurred. Two custodial officers and three inmates were killed. Fifteen officers and one inmate were wounded. The lives of hundreds of people were affected. Conditions on the island were never the same. Additional security measures were instituted, and the attitude of the dependent population toward the prisoners changed dramatically. In fact, one inmate assigned to an outside work detail actually lost his mind and had to be transferred to the U.S. Medical Center at Springfield, Missouri, because the island children were afraid and would no longer talk to him.

Hubbard's body was claimed by his wife and shipped to Alabama for burial. Cretzer's former wife, Edna, claimed his body and had him cremated at

Cypress Lawn Cemetery just south of San Francisco. Coy's body went unclaimed. He was buried at a local cemetery at government expense.

The repairs to the cell house required weeks to complete. C Block was uninhabitable due to the destruction of utility lines in the utility corridor. The inmates from C Block were temporarily housed in the hastily reconditioned A Block cells. Approximately thirty inmates were transferred to other penal institutions so Alcatraz could continue to house only one man in each cell.

The three surviving would-be escapees were charged with first-degree murder by the U.S. attorney in the death of William Miller. They were not charged with killing Stites. Since Cretzer had done the shooting, the defendants were accused of aiding and abetting Cretzer in the killing and with conspiracy to commit murder. The prosecution asked the jury for the death penalty for all three.

After a five-week trial in federal district court in San Francisco, all three were found guilty. The jury directed that Thompson and Shockley be executed. Because of his youth and the efforts he made to save the lives of the hostages, the jury spared Carnes's life. He received another life sentence.

The death sentences were appealed to both the Ninth Circuit Court of Appeals and the U.S. Supreme Court. Both courts affirmed the sentences. On December 3, 1948, Thompson and Shockley were executed simultaneously in the gas chamber at San Quentin Prison. By law, federal executions are carried out in accordance with the law of the state in which the sentence is ordered. San Quentin is the site of California executions. The prison is located in Marin County on the north shore of San Francisco Bay. Marin County was the contemplated landing point of the would-be Alcatraz escapees.

Among the official witnesses to the executions were three Alcatraz officers—Robert Baker, Frank Johnson, and Joe Steere—all of whom had played active roles in quelling the escape attempt. As the two men in the gas chamber took their first breath of the deadly cyanide gas, their heads slumped forward on their chests. When it was announced that both men were dead, Baker remarked, "That makes it five of them to two of us. It's a little more even now."

Afterword

The only would-be escapee not to die in the battle or in the gas chamber, Joe Carnes, was returned to Alcatraz after his trial and placed in isolation. There he remained for more than six years. He was assigned a cell next to Robert Stroud, with whom he became friends. Stroud was an excellent chess player. The two played every day. Each man maintained a board and two complete chess sets and called out the moves and positions of the various pieces. By the time he returned to the general prison population, Carnes was an accomplished chess player and reigned as prison champion for more than ten years.

In January 1963, just four months before Alcatraz was closed, Carnes was transferred to the medical center in Springfield, Missouri, for gallbladder surgery. He was thirty-six years old and had served twenty years in prison, seventeen and a half of those years on Alcatraz.

Following his surgery, Carnes was transferred to Leavenworth. There, he worked at various clerical jobs and comported himself as a model prisoner. He earned a high-school equivalency certificate and completed several college courses.

In 1974, Carnes was paroled to the custody of his sister in Kansas City, Missouri. He had weathered some of the toughest prisons in America, but the middle-aged Choctaw could not survive "on the outside." He found the free life lonely, frightening, and overwhelming. Unable to cope with his new status, Carnes intentionally violated his parole in 1976 so he could return to prison. He served an additional eighteen months in Leavenworth and was paroled again in 1978.

In 1979, Carnes's autobiography was purchased by a Hollywood production company and developed into a two-part television movie. Carnes was hired as a consultant and was paid $20,000. He spent several months on Hollywood sound stages and on location at Alcatraz. The movie Alcatraz—The Whole Shocking Story aired in 1980.

By that time Carnes's money had been frittered away on high living, alcohol, and unpaid loans to friends. His health began to fail. He slipped into the oblivion of life on the Kansas City streets. He lived in halfway houses, vacant buildings, and on the street until his alcohol-ravaged body gave out. Suffering from diabetes and numerous other medical disorders, he was again confined in the medical fa-

cility in Springfield. An entry in his file made Febru-
ary 2, 1987, summarized his status:

> *Carnes remains very much an institutional-
> ized individual. He suffers from alcoholism,
> diabetes, and loneliness. He has most recently
> stated that he wants to die in a Federal Penal
> Institution rather than an old folks' home.
> Carnes states he will refuse any release from
> parole. He has little else but the Federal System
> to live in and for. Carnes has great difficulty
> adjusting to community living. Carnes is no
> threat to anyone but himself. I believe he is as
> stable as he ever will be. Prison is home.*

Joe Carnes died of AIDS at the U.S. Medical Center for Federal Prisoners in Springfield, Missouri, in
1988 at the age of 61.

Ernie Lageson continued as an Alcatraz custodial
officer until January 1948, when he resigned to re-
sume his career as an educator. He became a high-
school biology and history teacher in Pittsburg, California. In Pittsburg, Eunice taught in one of the
elementary schools. Young Ernie attended Pittsburg
High School.

In secondary education Lageson was able to do
what he could not do at Alcatraz: have a meaningful,
positive impact on the lives of others. He was one of
the most respected teachers in the school. His "vel-
vet-fisted" discipline turned around the lives of several young men who, without his counsel and guidance, may well have ended up like Thompson and
Carnes.

In 1952, Ernie Lageson became assistant principal and dean of boys at Pittsburg Junior High School. He died of cancer in the summer of 1953 at the age of forty-two.

Eunice Lageson remarried in 1956. She married Don Martin, who had trained with Ernie when they first became guards at Alcatraz. Ernie and Don had been best friends. Martin's wife Elnora had died the previous year. Eunice and Don are now retired and living in northern California.

Ernie Lageson Jr. graduated from the University of California in 1954 and served as a commissioned officer in the Navy before entering the Boalt Hall School of Law at the University of California, Berkeley. He became a trial lawyer, practicing in San Francisco and Walnut Creek, California, until his retirement in 1993.

Of the other hostages, Robert Baker recovered from his wounds and returned to Alcatraz, where he worked until his retirement. He continued to reside north of San Francisco in Marin County and, upon retirement, developed an interest in the wine industry. He accepted employment with the Almaden Winery in St. Helena, California, where he worked until his death.

Following the riot, Phillip Bergen was appointed captain of the guards, a post he held for several years. He left the island after serving there for sixteen years. He subsequently served as a correctional inspector with the Federal Bureau of Prisons and as associate warden at the federal correctional institution at La Tuna, Texas. Now in his nineties, he is retired and lives in Arizona. He makes an annual visit to Alcatraz to speak at the Alcatraz Anniversary Weekend.

Several other hostages stayed at Alcatraz until retirement. Many took more peaceful jobs after retirement. Robert Bristow went to work as a custodian in the Sacramento School District. He and his wife Irene lived in the Sacramento area until their deaths. Gun-gallery guard Bert Burch moved to Arizona, where he lived with his son Dean until his death. Joe Burdett moved to a retirement community near Davis, California, where he lived until his death. Frank Johnson, who was on duty in the Main Tower when the riot began and was involved in the capture of the west gun gallery, also lived in Davis. Carl Sundstrom continued to live in San Francisco after retiring and maintained contact with his many friends on Alcatraz Island. He suffered a fatal stroke after several years in retirement.

Following a lengthy period of convalescence and rehabilitation, Cecil Corwin returned to duty. Several years later he was investigated for allegedly carrying unauthorized letters out of the prison for inmates. Soon after the investigation began, Corwin retired and the matter was dropped. He and his wife moved to Stockton, California, and later to Long Beach, California, where he resided until his death.

Of the administrative staff, Armorer Cliff Fish continued on at Alcatraz as the armory officer until his retirement. He presently lives in northern California.

Associate Warden E.J. "Jughead" Miller retired in 1947. He and his wife returned to their home in Leavenworth, Kansas, where he began his career in the federal prison service thirty years earlier. He was in failing health and struggled with diabetes and a serious heart condition. He died soon after retiring.

Because of his wounds, Lieutenant Joseph Simpson never returned to active duty. He received a medical retirement. He and his wife moved to Leavenworth, Kansas, where they lived until their deaths.

Also because of his wounds, Captain Henry Weinhold was never able to return to work. He received a medical retirement and moved to San Diego with his wife to be near their daughter. He died of a heart attack in 1967.

Warden James A. Johnston retired in April 1948 at the age of seventy-four, while the appeals of Shockley and Thompson were still pending. He was then appointed by President Harry Truman to the U.S. Board of Parole, where he served for several years as one of the board's most distinguished and effective parole judges. Johnston died in San Francisco at the age of eighty-four.

By 1962, the end of Alcatraz—the prison—was at hand. The facility needed physical repairs that would cost the government millions. And, with operation costs at six million dollars a year, it was already expensive to keep going. So, on May 15, 1963, seventeen years after the bloody outbreak of 1946, Alcatraz Island Prison was officially closed. Many of the inmates were transferred to the new federal maximum-security facility in Marion, Illinois.

Today Alcatraz is part of the U.S. Department of the Interior, National Park Service. It is a property within the Golden Gate National Recreation Area and is operated as a national park and museum. Approximately 1.5 million visitors each year tour the island and its remaining structures.

During the twenty-eight years Alcatraz functioned as a federal prison, a total of thirty-four inmates took part in fourteen escape attempts. (Since Cretzer & Shockley were both involved in two escape attempts, the actual number of attempted escapees was thirty-six.) Of this total, twenty-three were recaptured within a short time, seven were killed by gunfire from custodial officers, one drowned, and five disappeared without a trace in the frigid, swirling waters of the bay. No prisoner is ever known to have escaped from Alcatraz and lived.

Other Resources on Alcatraz

Campbell, Bruce J. *A Farewell to The Rock: Escape From Alcatraz*. New York: McGraw-Hill, 1963.

Clark, Howard. *Six Against The Rock*. New York: The Dial Press, 1977.

DeNevi, Don. *Alcatraz '46: The Anatomy of a Classic Prison Tragedy*. San Rafael, Calif.: Leswing Press, 1977.

Gaddis, Thomas E. *Birdman of Alcatraz*. New York: Random House, 1955.

Gardner, Roy. *Hellcatraz, The Rock of Despair*. Hearst Publishing, 1939.

Godwin, John. *Alcatraz: 1868-1963*. Garden City, N.Y.: Doubleday & Co., 1963.

Heaney, Frank. *Inside the Walls of Alcatraz*. Palo Alto, Calif.: Bull Publishing, 1978.

Hurley, Donald J. *Alcatraz Island: Boyhood Memories*. Sonoma, Calif.: [Self-published], 1987.

_____. *Alcatraz Island: Maximum Security*. Sonoma, Calif.: Fog Bell Enterprises, 1989.

Johnston, James A. *Alcatraz Island Prison and the Men Who Live There*. New York: Charles Scribner's Sons, 1949.

Justice Department. Bureau of Prisons. *Gearing Federal Prisons to the War Effort*. Atlanta: U.S. Penitentiary, 1942.

_____. *The Bulletin Board*. Vol. VIII No. 26. Washington, D.C., 1946.

_____. *The United States Penitentiary of Alcatraz Island, California*. (pamphlet) Atlanta: U.S. Penitentiary, 1952.

Karpis, Alvin. *On The Rock: Twenty-Five Years in Alcatraz*. New York: Beaufort Books, 1979.

Odier, Pierre. *The Rock: A History of Alcatraz, The Fort/The Prison*. Eagle Rock, Calif.: L'lmarge Odier Publishing, 1982.

Quillan, Jim. *Alcatraz From Inside*. San Francisco: Golden Gate National Park Association, 1991.

Online Resources

Golden Gate National Recreation Area
www.nps.gov/alcatraz

Alcatraz – History, Archives, Links
www.notfrisco.com/alcatraz

Alcatraz Gazette Online
www.geocities.com/marguerite_b/Prison/prison.html

About the Author

Ernest B. Lageson is a retired attorney, having practiced law in California for thirty-four years. Lageson graduated from the University of California at Berkeley Boalt Hall School of Law in 1959. He also received a bachelor of science degree in business administration from Berkeley. Lageson spent two years in the U.S. Navy. He began his career as a deputy district attorney in Contra Costa County. In 1961 he joined the San Francisco law firm Bronson, Bronson & McKinnon as a civil-trial lawyer. Over the next twenty-five years, he became nationally recognized for his work in civil-jury and nonjury cases. He was invited into such prestigious trial lawyer organizations as the American College of Trial Lawyers, the American Board of Trial Advocates, and the International Association of Defense Counsel. In 1986, Lageson served as president of the Defense

Research Institute, a national trial lawyer organization with a membership of 20,000.

Later, Lageson concluded his active legal career as a partner with Archer, McComas & Lageson in Walnut Creek, California, again trying civil-jury cases. He retired in 1992.

Lageson and his wife Jeanne make their home in the San Francisco Bay Area. They have two grown children, Kristine Cardall and Ernest B. Lageson III, and four grandchildren.

Ernie Lageson may be reached by e-mail. His address: lagesoneb@aol.com

Addicus Books
Visit the Addicus Books Web Site
http://www.addicusbooks.com

On the Back Roads —
Discovering Small Towns of America   *$16.95*
    Bill Graves / 1-886039-36-4

The ABCs of Gold Investing   *$14.95*
    Michael Kosares / 1-886039-29-1

Battle at Alcatraz —
A Desperate Attempt to Escape the Rock   *$16.95*
    Ernest Lageson / 1-886039-37-2

Counterpoint: A Murder in Massachusetts Bay   *$16.95*
    Margaret Press / 1-886039-24-0

Eye of the Beast   *$16.95*
    Terry Adams / 1-886039

The Family Compatibility Test   *$9.95*
    Susan Adams / 1-886039-27-5

First Impressions: Tips to Enhance Your Image   *$14.95*
    Joni Craighead / 1-886039-26-7

The Healing Touch—Keeping the Doctor/Patient
Relationship Alive Under Managed Care   *$9.95*
    David Cram, MD / 1-886039-31-3

Hello, Methuselah! Living to 100 and Beyond   *$14.95*
    George Webster, PhD / 1-886039-25-9

Prescription Drug Abuse: The Hidden Epidemic   *$14.95*
    Rod Colvin / 1-886039-22-4

Simple Changes:
The Boomer's Guide to a Healthier, Happier Life   *$9.95*
    L. Joe Porter, MD / 1-886039-35-6

Straight Talk About Breast Cancer   *$12.95*
    Suzanne Braddock, MD / 1-886039-21-6

The Street-Smart Entrepreneur   *$14.95*
    Jay Goltz / 1-886039-33-X

The Stroke Recovery Book   *$14.95*
    Kip Burkman, MD / 1-886039-30-5

Suddenly Gone   *$15.95*
    Dan Mitrione / 1-886039-23-2

Understanding Postpartum Depression and Anxiety   *$12.95*
    Linda Sebastian, RN / 1-886930-34-8

Please send:

_____ copies of _____

(Title of book)

at $ _____ each   TOTAL   _____

Nebr. residents add 5% sales tax   _____

Shipping/Handling
   $3.00 for first book.
   $1.00 for each additional book.   _____

         TOTAL ENCLOSED   _____

Name _____

Address _____

City _____ State _____ Zip _____

☐ Visa   ☐ Master Card   ☐ Am. Express

Credit card number _____ Expiration date _____

Order by credit card, personal check or money order.

Send to:
   Addicus Books
   Mail Order Dept.
   P.O. Box 45327
   Omaha, NE 68145

Or, order **TOLL FREE: 800-352-2873**